THE COMPLETE BOOK OF
TROUT
FLYFISHING

THE COMPLETE BOOK OF TROUT FLY-FISHING has been originated, produced and designed by AB Nordbok, Gothenburg, Sweden.

Editorial chief: Göran Cederberg
Designer: Thommy Gustavsson
Setting: Designia
Translator: Jon van Leuven
Illustrations: Thommy Gustavsson, Gunnar Johnson

Nordbok would like to express sincere thanks to all others who have contributed in different ways to the production of this book.

Photography

Sune Adolfsson: pages 32, 33, 35, 44-45, 94, 137
Erwin Bauer: pages 61, 131 (inset), 135, 168, 182-183
Björn Blomqvist: pages 28-29, 64, 65, 124-125, 179, 187
Bill Browning: pages 9, 13, 82-83
Mikael Engström: cover (inset) and pages 10-11, 14-15, 110-111, 136-137, 181
Thommy Gustavsson: pages 102-103, 184
Jens Ploug Hansen: pages 6, 13, 19 (inset), 21, 59, 105, 163, 169, 176-177
Hainz Jagusch: pages 19, 22-23, 39, 41, 57 (top), 122, 138, 139
Pelle Klippinge: pages 18, 38, 52, 152-153, 172-173
Steen Larsen: pages 18 (inset), 21, 115, 131, 154-155, 161, 166-167, 180, 185
Sören Lindrot: cover and pages 3, 32, 50, 56, 57 (bottom), 62-63, 89, 106-107, 127
Ulf Pierrou: pages 42, 43

THE COMPLETE BOOK OF
TROUT
FLYFISHING

SWAN·HILL
PRESS

The Authors

GÖRAN CEDERBERG, the editor of this book, has planned it and edited the contributors' texts with adaptation for an international audience. An enthusiastic, experienced flyfisherman and a regular contributor to European sportfishing publications, he is chief editor of the journal "Sportfiske-magasinet ESOX". Among other large international book projects, he has edited Nordbok's "Complete Book of Sportfishing" and "Complete Book of Flyfishing". Göran Cederberg has written the Introduction and Chapter 6.

THOMMY GUSTAVSSON is a graphic designer, illustrator, and nature painter as well as a dedicated flyfisherman. For many years he has contributed articles and illustrations to mainly Scandinavian sportfishing publications and several books on fishing. Thommy Gustavsson is responsible for both the design of this book and most of its illustrations.

GUNNAR JOHNSON is known primarily as an artist in the fields of fishing, wildlife and nature, through his illustrations of books and magazines both in Scandinavia and elsewhere. He is also editor of the magazine "Flugfiske i Norden" (Flyfishing in Scandinavia) and has written or contributed to many books, mainly on classic flyfishing. Gunnar Johnson has written Chapters 2-5 and created a large number of the book's illustrations.

STEEN ULNITS is a fishing journalist who specializes in flyfishing. He contributes to European sportfishing magazines and has written several books on fish biology, flyfishing and flytying, among others. His experience with flyfishing covers almost all corners of the world. Steen Ulnits has written Chapters 1, 7 and 8.

Contents

An Introduction to Trout Flyfishing

*E*ven though this is meant to be a complete book about trout flyfishing, we shall use the term "trout" in its widest sense. At first, one naturally thinks of the classic trout of river and stream; but there are related fish that regularly migrate out to sea, and those that inhabit inland lakes. Sea trout and lake trout belong to the same biological species as brown trout - yet they have adapted during thousands of years to the possibilities of survival offered by the environment.

When the family circle is widened further, other adipose-finned relatives like rainbow trout, char and grayling are included as "trout". Thus, while the following pages describe flyfishing mainly in terms of brown trout, fishing for their family members and close relatives will also be discussed on occasion.

Trout and the joy of fishing

To many of us, fishing for trout with a fly and fly-rod is a way of living, and a manner of keeping in touch with life and nature. Regardless of which waters we choose to wet our flies in – from the bank of a fine peaceful stream, from a belly boat out on a shining lake, or perhaps simply from a boat along the coast – we engage in a kind of fishing that can be difficult and frustrating, as well as extremely enjoyable and exciting.

Certainly I do not want to argue that a trout flyfisher-man experiences greater luck than other fishermen, however much I would love to believe it. Good fortune in fishing may imply big fish and great catches, but can at least as often embrace everything that goes with the fishing and gives the fisherman satisfaction. One example is the beauty of natural scenery. Another is the deeper contact with, and understanding of, the ecological system's impressive diversity and perfection, which we acquire at fishing waters. There is also the feeling of harmony and wholeness in seeing the fly, after a superb cast, land exactly on the rings left by a rising trout – and watching it rise again, an instant later, to take the artificial insect.

Trout and nature

Since trout are both sensitive and fastidious fish, they place strong demands upon their surroundings. As a result, they cannot be found in any old sewer. What they require is clean, fresh water with a relatively high pH value, and they usually live on food that exists only in a virtually unspoiled environment.

In addition, being a shy and vigilant creature, the trout is frequently not a little skeptical of our artificial, more or less well-tied, flies. All this makes trout flyfishing a thrilling, and sometimes very complex, art.

Whichever one's reasons for beginning to fish trout, it can be said with confidence that the trout flyfisher-

man is indeed a fortunate individual, because he or she has the benefit of lingering in the same ambience as the trout: in scenic and possibly quite wild, pristine regions that, like an oasis, impart happiness and provide a watering-hole for the soul.

Trout and equipment

Granted that trout should never be underestimated in their ability to see through our insect imitations, we have to keep in mind that sportfishing in general – and flyfishing in particular – is primarily a sport for pleasure. Consequently, the fishing must not be made any harder than necessary, and this applies especially to the choice of equipment.

All too many flyfishermen, notably those who regard trout flyfishing as a mere whim of fashion, imagine that the equipment is what determines whether or not fish are caught. It is quite wrong to assume that your fishing luck will be proportional to the price of your gear; an expensive and exclusive outfit does not mean that you have bought a guarantee of getting fish. As with every type of fishing, a trout flyfisherman's success depends more on knowledge of nature, of how the fish react to different stimuli, and of when or where to present them with flies, than on the equipment used.

Trout and the fisherman

Most trout flyfishermen are doubtless in full agreement that the basic goal of this sport is rarely to catch either as many, or as large, fish as possible. Though exceptions always occur, one might .even claim that the average trout flyfisherman is something of a philosopher. He or she is often a calm, rather reserved person with a surprising degree of patience, good at observing the surroundings, careful and watchful, far from impulsive and seldom easy to fool – just like the trout.

Therefore, in order to outwit trout, an adept flyfisherman ought to possess the very qualities that characterize the quarry. A big old, hard-to-conquer trout would not have survived so long if it lacked any of the above-mentioned traits. Being able to put oneself in the trout's position, and to act on this basis, is an essential ingredient in the recipe that leads a trout flyfisherman to triumph.

Trout and life

Challenging trout in their true natural element is, I maintain, among the richest sources of excitement to be found on earth. An entire lifetime can be spent at the same fishing waters without becoming completely skilled in the sport.

It may take years to discover the fish's holding places, still longer to learn entomology, and yet more time to achieve a correct presentation of the fly. Once you have mastered, for instance, dry-fly and wet-fly and nymph fishing, you can start exploring how to tie flies with the right materials. Then comes a refinement of casting techniques, until you take up building rods of split cane. To be sure, each of us decides how far, and in what sequence, to develop an interest in flyfishing; but the vast range of opportunities is the fascinating thing about it. And the trout remain as irresistibly tempting as they are elusive.

No matter how lucky one is in the art of fishing with a fly and fly-rod, how great a share of one's life it commands, and whether or not one considers trout flyfishing to be the most important of one's activities, it can be a comfort to realize that the alternatives would probably not have been half as much fun. This insight is the driving force behind our attempts, day after day and year after year, to attract the next trout to take an artificial fly. It is also why we never lose hope of someday getting to know our dear friend, the trout.

Trout flyfishing is a refreshing as well as pleasant pastime. Since wild trout place rather strict demands upon their environment, they lead the fisherman into beautiful surroundings with relatively clean water. For many of us, this is the essential charm of the sport.

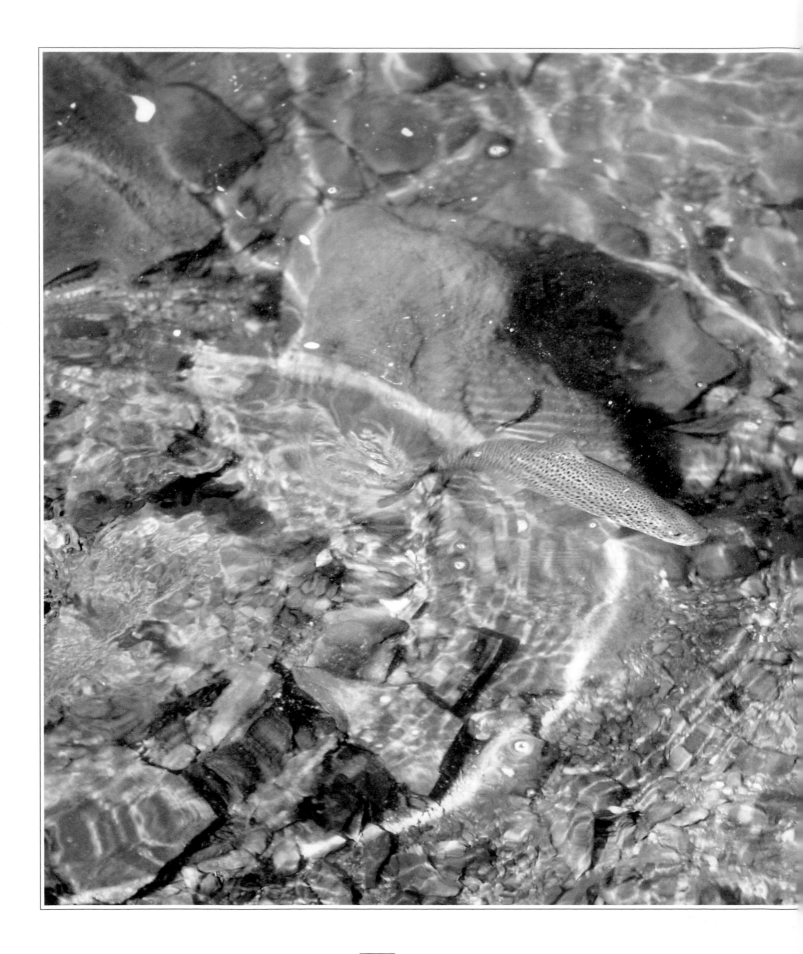

Trout and their Habitats

The creatures we call fish have a long history of evolution – about 450 million years of it. Those that live today are normally divided into three main groups: round–mouthed fish, cartilaginous fish, and bony fish. The first group includes hagfishes; examples of the second group are sharks and rays. Bony fish are a vast group that now boasts over 30,000 species, and among them we find the salmonoids, such as trout.

Adipose-finned fish

Characteristic of a salmonoid is its small, rudimentary, adipose fin, located between the dorsal and tail fins. This is not, however, confined to the true salmonoids, since some other and quite unrelated fish – from the Southern Hemisphere, where no original salmonoids exist – have corresponding adipose fins. The name of the family Salmonidae apparently derives from a Latin word *salire* meaning "leap", which refers to several of its species' ability to get past high waterfalls on their migrations.

Few species and many variations

Another typical trait of salmonoids is their amazing capacity for occurring in diverse colours. For instance, strains of trout often have such different colour markings that they were once thought to represent distinct species. Today we know that there are only a small number of species, yet consisting of countless variants.

In addition, the salmonoids frequently occur in both stationary and migrating forms. Sea trout, lake-run trout, and brown trout were previously regarded as three separate species, but they have turned out to be just contrasting forms of the same species – the European trout. Whether a particular trout

becomes the first, second, or third of these forms is determined partly by its heredity, and partly by external factors.

Migrations

Salmonoids commonly migrate for very long distances. These may be limited to the water system in which they were born, or may extend over vast stretches of ocean. Two kinds of migrations can be recognized by their purposes: to find food or to spawn.

Spawning migrations are undertaken by the great majority of salmonoids, which do not live at their spawning places. When the spawning season approaches, the mature fish begin to migrate toward spawning grounds in the smaller tributaries, usually lying upstream rather than downstream.

Trout that spend all their lives in lakes or rivers seldom need to make extreme migrations, the usual length being a couple of kilometres. Seagoing rainbow trout, or "steelhead", on the other hand, may wander for several thousand kilometres across the open sea before returning to their spawning river.

Food migrations have a different character. Their natural basis is the search for nourishment. Thus, what attract the fish are regions in which they can find the most food. Small sea trout often stay near the mouths of the waterways they were hatched in, satisfying their preference for crustaceans, ragworms and various little fish. The larger sea trout, though, gladly strike out into open waters and follow schools of herring or elvers.

Where the fish grow up

The spawning grounds used by salmonoids are too restricted in area to hold any sizeable stocks of adult fish. This is because the food supplies are insufficient. Consequently, many salmonoids have developed a

Trout inhabit diverse environments in many parts of the world - from fast currents in rough mountain country to slow streams and rivers in fertile plains. (Above left) This type of trout water is often found in mountainous highlands, shown here in North America. (Above right) A nutritious lowland stream, like this one in New Zealand, may have good stocks of fine trout. (Below right) In an American spring creek, the water flows calmly and smoothly.

suitable life cycle: their spawning places are populated only during a short period of the year by adults, which then eat almost nothing. For the rest of the year, these places serve simply as growth areas of the young fish. As the latter develop, they swim ever farther away from the spawning grounds. Finally, if they belong to migrant species, they depart into a lake or the sea. There, both space and food for large stocks of adult fish are available.

It is also typical that the trout which return, ready to spawn, eat very little food while in fresh waters. Instead, they live on the reserves of fat which they have accumulated at sea. This is still another wonderful example of adaptation, since even a modest number of large adult fish would be enough to diminish all the food in a waterway – to the serious disadvantage of their own offspring.

In sum, salmonoids exploit the best virtues of two worlds: the security of gravel bottoms in flowing waters, and the opportunities of growth in lakes and seas.

Spawning

Most salmonoids spawn in waters that are flowing. The fish lay eggs in pits which are dug by the females on gravel bottoms. After her eggs are laid and fertilized, the female covers them with gravel, forming another pit in the process.

If all goes well, the eggs hatch some months later. The fry have characteristic yolk-sacs and, once these are consumed, will find their way up through the gravel. After leaving the bottom, they are more mobile and, at the same time, less vulnerable. For the fertilized eggs, lying buried in the bottom, are very sensitive to flooding and desiccation, silt and other external influences on the environment.

When spawning, trout do not need very deep water to lay their ova in. But the spawning beds or redds must have a suitable current speed and bottom structure, with no risk of drainage or drought.

Special requirements

Salmonoids are cold-water fish, which need good water quality with a high oxygen content. If the water quality declines, or if spawning places are destroyed, their stock of salmonoids will therefore quickly die out. The same happens if the fish are prevented from gaining access to their vital spawning grounds, as when we build hydroelectric plants or culverts on the spawning waterways.

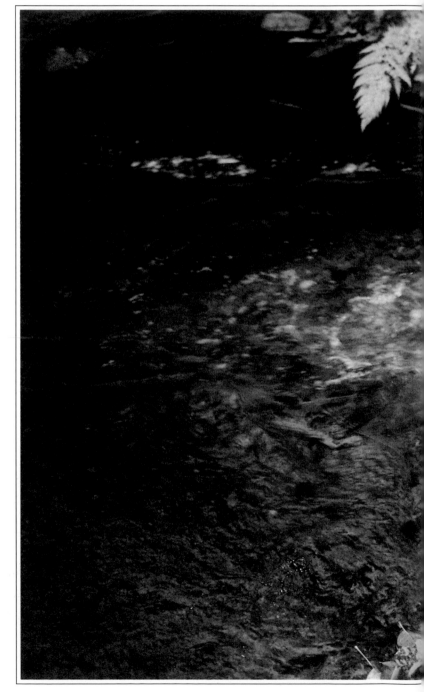

The fish do not adopt spawning places at random: these must fulfil particular demands. Such places occur where the bottoms have an appropriate structure, and where the current speed is right. River beds of gravel or stone with a moderate water flow are chosen. Brook trout (squaretail) and landlocked Arctic char, as well as the "true" trout, are exceptions that prove the rule. They can also spawn in cold lakes and other still waters with clean stony beds. Here they are unable, of course, to dig pits;

but instead the female sweeps the eggs down into crevices between boulders.

Threats to the fish

Construction of dams, and especially of hydroelectric plants, is the single factor that has had the greatest negative impact on stocks of wild salmonoids. It is naturally impossible for the fish to force the dam banks – unless these are equipped with a well-function-

ing salmon pass, which is unfortunately often not the case. The result is that the fish cannot reach their spawning places.

Moreover, dams are usually built on the stretches of river that have the greatest fall in height, since electricity production can be maximized there. But it is in those very areas that the salmonoids have their main spawning grounds. Even the operation of a hydroelectric plant may affect the fish stocks quite negatively. The water is frequently collected slowly in a reservoir, to be released quickly through turbines – so the water level is constantly rising and falling. This does essential harm to the living conditions for fish, as large regions are regularly laid dry and later reflooded. The turbines themselves are responsible for killing millions of outward-migrating young salmon and trout, which are sucked into them and hacked to pieces.

Territories

From the moment when a tiny salmonoid first looks up from its gravel bottom, until the day it migrates out to a lake or sea, it maintains a territory that it defends aggressively against intruding relatives.

While the fish are small, their primary need is to secure a holding place where they can find protection and plenty of food. Some form of *current lee* is also necessary. However, when there is no current to take account of – in lakes and seas – the fish seldom have any true holding places or territories, since both space and food are abundant.

But after returning as mature adult fish, they are all the more territorial. Then they compete once again for the best holding places, although no longer because of food. The females want to get the best spawning sites, and the males want the best females.

Changes in colouring

In streams and rivers, the small salmonoids have a dark silver hue, which gives them excellent camouflage against the bottom stones. Nevertheless, it is unsuitable for life in the open water of lakes and seas. Trout that intend to migrate into such waters must, therefore, disguise themselves as fry.

Just before departing, they acquire a silver-shiny

hunting appearance. This provides good camouflage in the free water masses. The little "fry" grow rapidly in a lake or sea, until at a certain point – normally after one or two years – they become sexually mature and swim back to the waterway in order to spawn.

Often the fish return in their silvery hunting costume with a thin skin and loose scales, but soon take on a vivid spawning dress with a tough skin and a thick, protective layer of mucus. The males also develop a powerfully hooked kelp, which makes them look fierce and can frighten away potential rivals from the spawning place.

The spawning trout lay their ova on sandy or gravelly bottoms with an adequate flow of water (above right). Below, we see a trout fry with its yolk-sac, and a young trout that has become silvery. This change occurs just before migrating into a lake or the sea, for good camouflage in the free water. Farthest down is a pair of trout in their vivid mating colours, which promote the survival of the species.

Recovering strength

As the time for spawning draws near, the males in particular show increasing aggression towards each other – as well as increasing interest in the roe-filled females. Now the females seek out the best spawning sites and dig the first pits. When everything is ready, the females lay their eggs, which the males soon fertilize.

Once all the eggs are laid and covered, the fish are tired and emaciated. They head for the current lees, so as to regain their energy. Being thus spawned out,

with their stores of fat converted into water, they are thin and virtually inedible. Spawning fish that are caught should always be released.

The fish that have travelled farthest to reach their spawning grounds are in very poor condition after spawning, and many of them die from these exertions. Yet given a chance, the majority recuperate quickly, and will return the next winter to take part in the spawning activities.

The species of salmonoids

When we speak of flyfishing for trout, we often mean flyfishing not only for "real" trout but also for char and grayling. Though they are all salmonoids, it is important to know the differences between them. The "real" trout are characterized by black spots on a light background. These include both the European trout *Salmo trutta* and the North American rainbow trout *Salmo gairdneri* The Arctic char *Salvelinus alpinus* and the eastern brook trout *Salvelinus fontinalis* however, are not "real" trout but char, with light spots on a dark background.

Characteristic of the grayling is an outsized dorsal fin, largest on the male. There are two species, the European grayling *Thymallus thymallus* and the Arctic *Thymallus arcticus*.

Trout

European trout are distributed across Eurasia and in North Africa. Despite their close relationship to the Atlantic salmon, which occurs on both sides of the North Atlantic, trout are not found naturally in North America – they were brought by man during the late 1800s.

As mentioned earlier, *Salmo trutta* exists in three distinct forms: the seagoing trout *Salmo trutta trutta*, lake-run trout *Salmo trutta lacustris* and brown trout *Salmo trutta fario*. All of these are very active at night – more so than other salmonoids – and are more strongly inclined to have a "roof above their heads", such as an overhanging branch or a hollowed-out shore bank.

Sea trout

There are considerable contrasts between sea trout in regard to how far they migrate and how fast they grow. In water with a high salt content, they do not make distant journeys like salmon. To be sure, they do so in the brackish Baltic Sea, which is an almost ideal environment for sea trout, and yields specimens of more than 15 kg (33 lbs). But under perfect conditions the lake-run trout seems to grow at least as well as its relatives in the sea. In fact, lake-run trout can become even bigger than sea trout, even if this happens infrequently.

Two trout with very different looks. There is a great contrast between the silvery fish before spawning and, some months later, its tired and coloured appearance.

Lake-run trout

Different forms of lake-run trout occur, and may vary greatly in appearance. Along shores, dark and speckled examples are often seen, living mainly on the bottom zone's insects and crustaceans – trout which rarely weigh much more than 1 kg (2.2 lbs). This is the type of lake trout that a flyfisherman usually encounters.

The free waters of large inland lakes, with their nutritious and exclusive fish diet, are inhabited by the really big, shiny silver lake trout. Also living in these waters is a little silvery variant that, instead, has specialized itself on plankton – not, of course, the most nourishing of foods – and tends to weigh only a few hundred grams. Red-spotted brown trout are satisfied with the limited food supply in streams and rivers; they seldom become heavier than 5 kg (11 lbs) and specimens of 1-2 kg (2.2-4.4 lbs) are counted as fine.

Rainbow trout

Found across western North America, from Alaska to Mexico, the rainbow trout *Salmo gairdneri* is distinguished by its pink gill-covers and red lateral line. A close relative is the smaller, but often more colourful, cutthroat trout *Salmo clarkii*, with a clear red slash on its throat. Both species have a densely spotted tail fin.

Like the European trout, rainbow trout occur in a seagoing form, a lake-living form, and one that is stationary in waterways. These, too, were once thought to be different species, but today we know better. The seagoing form, called a "steelhead", may weigh up to 20 kg (44 lbs). This size is normally reached after four years at sea – a rate of growth comparable with that of Atlantic salmon, to which steelhead are widely compared. But unlike all other, winter–spawning members of the genus *Salmo*, the rainbow spawns in springtime.

Rainbow trout exist in several variants: one that lives stationary in flowing waters, another inhabiting lakes, and a seagoing form known as the steelhead.

Over the Atlantic

In 1864 the first trout farm was started in the state of New York, to raise native eastern brook trout. Six years later, once the railroad network was fully built, a great manipulation of nature (or faunal pollution) began to take place. Efforts succeeded at transporting another species, the rainbow trout, from the country's wild Northwest to the populous east coast.

The initial shipments of rainbow trout reached the Atlantic seaboard in good condition. From there it was not hard to cross the ocean as well. A technique for bringing trout eggs over long distances had been learned. Eastern brook trout came to Europe already in 1879, and more exactly to Germany – followed within two years by rainbow trout. Then both species were spread to large parts of Europe; for instance, rainbow trout entered Sweden just before the turn of the century.

Restricted farming

European trout were later sent from Germany in the opposite direction. Even today, these fish are called "German browns" at many places in North America. They had previously been farmed to some extent in their homelands, but the imported brook trout became the first species to be raised for purposes of sale in Europe.

However, this delicacy was quickly outcompeted by rainbow trout, which are much less demanding. They can tolerate higher water temperatures, live more densely in farm ponds, and grow faster – making them ideal fish for commercial production. For the same reasons, rainbow trout have proved to be the most popular fish for today's put-and-take waters, where ready-to-catch rainbows are set out and soon caught again.

Char

All members of the genus *Salvelinus* are termed chars, in contrast to the brown trout. This name is believed to derive from a Celtic word for "blood-coloured"; a similar name in Sweden refers to the fish's amazingly beautiful spawning costume.

The ordinary char *Salvelinus alpinus* occurs, like the majority of salmonoids, in both seagoing and stationary forms. Chars have a "circumpolar" distribution, in the Arctic region around the world.

Ice Age relics

Coastal areas are dominated by the seagoing form. It migrates to sea when the ice melts in May-June, and returns in July-August, so its growth season is very short. Moreover, in springtime the fish are spawned out and, before they can grow at all, must regain their lost fat. Since they could not survive in salt water at such low temperatures, the winter is always spent in fresh waters. And the food supply in cold fresh water is minimal.

The stationary freshwater form of char is found farther inland, where it cannot migrate to sea. At numerous places in the Alps – well beyond the normal southern border of this species – char exist as a survival from the last Ice Age. The same applies to stocks in deep, and thus ice-cold, lakes around Ireland, England and Scotland. Here the fish live so far down that a flyfisherman has no chance to get acquainted with them.

In many large lakes, the char maintain quite separate stocks, as regards their way of life and their spawning grounds. They still belong to the same species – the stationary form of *Salvelinus alpinus* – but to different strains, each with its own special genetic constitution.

Four strains at once

A single lake may contain up to four strains of char. First, the "big char" live as predators in deeper layers, hunting schools of small fish in the free waters. They weigh as much as 10 kg (22 lbs), which is also true for heavy examples of seagoing char.

The flyfisherman can very seldom, if ever, come to grips with such big char. Instead, he meets the more common form that lives in the coastal zone and inhabits many small lakes in the mountains. These char usually weigh under 2-3 kg (4.4-6.6 lbs); their diet consists primarily of insects and crustaceans. They often have reddish stomachs throughout the year.

The third form, a dark bottom-living "dwarf char", also lives in relatively shallow waters, but rarely exceeds a few hundred grams in weight. More abundant is the fourth form, "plankton char". This populates the free water masses, filtering planktonic organisms which are so small that none of our flies can imitate them. Silver and shiny, it seldom grows bigger than the dwarf char.

Landlocked char (above) occur in both a stationary and a seagoing form. Both live only in the Arctic areas of the world. Another typical cold-water fish is the eastern brook trout, or squaretail (left) from eastern North America. But it tolerates warmer water than the char and is less dependent on Arctic environments.

In general, char have a greater preference for small foods than do trout, which enjoy substantial mouthfuls. Therefore, char tend to be caught on comparatively small flies.

Eastern brook trout

Salvelinus fontinalis is an exclusively North American char, occurring in nature only within the eastern parts of that continent. It needs colder water than do European trout, but cannot take an Arctic climate as the ordinary char do. Thus it is also found farther south, where the warmer water is unsuitable for char.

Brook trout are recognizable by their marbled back, and by the usually numerous red and blue spots on their sides. In addition, they have a head that is fairly large for salmonoids. The mouth is adapted to short summers, when mice and lemmings are often on their menu.

This is a short-lived fish, seldom weighing more than 1 kg (2.2 lbs). In Labrador and Quebec, though, stocks exist that regularly produce examples of 3-4 kg (6.6-8.8 lbs). Brook trout are mainly freshwater fish; a seagoing form occurs but, as a rule, is smaller than 1-2 kg.

Grayling

Among flyfishermen in Europe, the grayling is a very popular quarry. For no other salmonoid has a diet so dependent on insects. Since it also habitually eats food on the water surface, it is something of a dry-fly fisherman's dream.

The wide distribution of grayling resembles that of *Salmo trutta*: it is absent only from Ireland, most of Scotland, Spain, Portugal and Italy. In Central Europe, grayling are regarded as such an exclusive catch that people speak of a waterway's "grayling region", which lies downstream from the mountainous "trout region". In effect, grayling need less fast-flowing water than do trout.

Grayling in northern and central Sweden are often found in both lakes and rivers. Around the inner parts of the Gulf of Bothnia, they commonly occur even in brackish waters near the coast.

A large dorsal fin

The grayling is actually a closer relative of whitefish than of char. Like the former, it has white flesh and large scales. But a unique characteristic is the colossal size of its dorsal fin, which is biggest on the male.

In contrast to the territorial trout, grayling are glad to live in modest schools of more or less equally sized fish. Large grayling, however, are typical loners. As for weight, grayling can go up to 4 kg (8.8 lbs) – but specimens over 2 kg are rather rare today, so a catch over 1 kg is considered admirable.

Grayling are the favourite of many dry-fly fisherman, as they usually take various insects on or near the surface. Their main characteristic is a large dorsal fin, which is somewhat bigger on males than on females. Natural stocks of grayling occur chiefly in Scandinavia and the Alpine regions, where they inhabit running waters with moderate currents. In some parts of Scandinavia, they are also found in lakes and in the brackish coastal waters of the Gulf of Bothnia.

The fish and their environment

Trout are cold-blooded, like all fish, which means that their body temperature adjusts to the surrounding water's temperature. What determines a fish's metabolism, and consequently its level of activity, is thus the water temperature. In cold water its metabolism is correspondingly low, and the fish does not need much food. It then hunts only to a limited extent and can be difficult for a flyfisherman to make contact with.

A critical level

Salmonoids are oxygen-demanding, cold-water fish. In water of very low temperatures, their metabolism almost stops and they drift into a torpid state with minimal energy consumption. As the temperature rises, their metabolism increases and whets their appetite. Yet at the same time, greater metabolism heightens their demand on the water's oxygen content. And water can hold ever less oxygen as its temperature rises. So above a certain level, not enough oxygen exists for salmonoids. This critical temperature is usually around 20° C (68° F) for the most tolerant species.

In flowing waters, the fish can compensate for lack of oxygen by finding places with a strong current. Along rapids and below waterfalls, the water is better oxygenated, and they know it. During high summer, one can thus often catch fish all the way up to the foaming surface layer. In wintertime, when their metabolism is low, they instead seek calmer places with a current lee, where they can hold with a minimal consumption of oxygen.

These possibilities are not available to the fish in still waters, such as lakes and the sea. There, a different rule applies: deep water is coldest in the summer and warmest in wintertime. During the spring and autumn, when the shallow waters at the surface and near coasts have a moderate temperature and oxygen content, the fish gather in them to find food.

Regulating the salt balance

In salt water, trout and char have to cope with another problem. They must be able to regulate the salt balance in their bodies and cells. This requires energy, which is generated by the body's metabolism. But if the water temperature becomes too low, metabolism cannot produce the amount of extra energy which is needed for such a balance.

The fish then has only two alternatives: to stay in salt water and die, or to head for a place with warmer or less salty water. Thus, salmonoids are rarely seen in coastal marine waters during hard winters. They move up into fresh waters to spend the winter, or seek coves and fjords with brackish waters.

Temperature and salinity help to guide the fish's behaviour and migrations. Light, and food supplies, are two other external factors of great importance for both the fish and the fisherman.

How light influences food

Sunlight is the cause of photosynthesis in plants, which in turn are the basis of food chains. Where there is light, there is food – and where there is food in natural waters, there are fish. This is a simple but often-overlooked relationship.

Shallow water normally contains much less food than deep water, which allows less light to penetrate and thus has worse conditions for food production. In photosynthesis, water plants build up organic material from solar energy and the water's nutritive salts. They also absorb carbon dioxide from the water, and release the oxygen that organisms require. If a body of fishing water is to be productive, it must therefore contain a certain quantity of nutritive salts. As long as these are supplied naturally, a balance exists and the water remains clear and food-rich.

Eutrophication

But if the nutritive salts are added by artificial means – such as sewage water channeled into lakes and seas – the balance is soon destroyed. Too many salts accumulate, creating a bloom of plankton algae, and the water becomes murky. This process of "eutrophication" makes the bottom silt up with sunken, dead algae. Then the area in question can definitely be counted out as fishing water. The bottom flora that fish food depends on are gone, and with them disappear the insects and crustaceans – which are valuable not only for the fish as food, but also for us, when we tie flies as imitations!

It follows that the flyfisherman should concentrate on places with shallow, clear, nutritious water of high pro-

ductivity – areas of lush bottom vegetation that gives insects and crustaceans a good life. Here one can regularly come into contact with fish seeking food.

Light-shy fish

On the other hand, salmonoids – and particularly trout – are afraid of light and do not enjoy hunting in shallow water by day. They know where the food is, but are happy to wait until sundown before gathering it. So the best time to fish in summertime is often during the night hours.

This is not true, however, in the winter when the water is colder than the fish's optimum temperature. Then they move into shallow areas, even at midday

when the light is strongest and makes the water warmest. Thus, in order to obtain life-giving heat, they ignore their own safety and may meet their fate if a fisherman is present.

Trout are light-shy and, therefore, decidedly nocturnal fish - especially during the warm season. By day, they often stand in shadows and deeper water, waiting until after sunset to hunt in shallow areas. Thus, in summertime, fishing at night gives the best chances of catching trout, when they seek food under cover of darkness.

The senses of fish

Fish employ all of their senses when seeking food. Like other bony fish, a trout can both see and hear, feel and taste. But it hunts for food primarily by using its sight, which is more developed than would otherwise be necessary. It is very sensitive to colours in the daytime, and can see in the dark much better than humans do. At night, though, a fish sees everything in black and white.

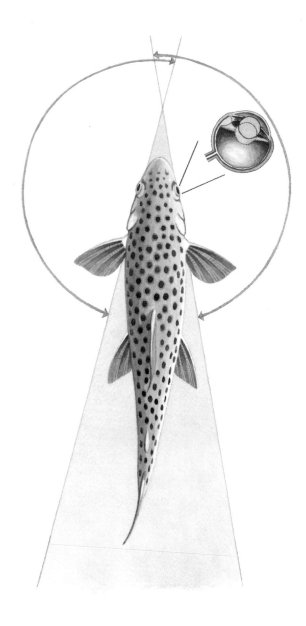

The eyes of fish have spherical lenses, and can be moved independently of each other, so they provide a very wide field of vision. Yet the field in which a fish can focus an object with both eyes is very narrow. As a result, the fish must react quickly to catch food in flowing waters.

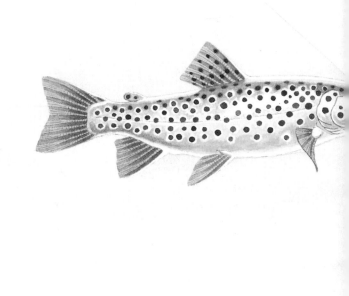

Sounds and the lateral line

In unclear water and during the night, a trout also commonly uses its well-developed lateral line in order to orient itself and locate prey. The lateral line is a kind of extended hearing-aid, an organ that mainly registers low-frequency sound waves underwater.

As the fish moves, it sends out pressure waves. If these strike objects in the water, they bounce back and the fish can detect them. The lateral line then acts like a sonar receiver. Similarly, a hunting trout can pick up movements from small fish that flee, or from other large food. This is especially helpful for discovering and catching prey in water with poor visibility.

The flyfisherman, too, may benefit at night by using sizeable flies, such as the larger Muddlers. They can send out sound waves in the water and can be heard as well as seen – by the fish!

In order to judge the distance to an insect – or to your fly – the fish must be able to focus on it. Fish can see up through the water surface through a cone-shaped field, with an angle of about 97.5 degrees. But the higher they are in the water, the smaller is the "window" area covered by this field at the surface, and the more quickly the fish must react. For a flyfisherman, this means the fly must be presented ever more precisely, and the fish have ever less time to be selective – especially in rapid waters.

A fish can detect low-frequency sound waves by means of its lateral line. At night and in murky waters, this provides the fish with a kind of sonar guidance. When fishing in darkness, one can use suitable flies, such as big noisy Muddlers, which are easiest for trout to identify and take.

Trout Flies
and their
Natural Models

To understand the special requirements of flyfishing, we need a basic acquaintance with insects and other small water-living animals, which are the models for our fishing flies. This does not mean that a flyfisherman must be able to distinguish every insect from the rest of its species, but he or she ought to be familiar enough with entomology – the science of insects – to know something about the life cycles of different insect groups and the demands they place on their respective environments, in order to tell where, when and how they occur.

Insect life in fishing waters

Every kind of insect has particular requirements for its living conditions, so that we meet different species in each type of water and at each time during the season. This, in turn, is naturally of great significance for our choice of fishing flies, depending on the time of year that we fish, and on whether we fish in still or flowing waters. Within a lake or waterway, too, insects vary between areas with distinctive environmental characteristics. Some species flourish in strongly turbulent water, while others prefer places with weaker currents, or even calmly moving pools.

Moreover, the insect fauna changes in composition through the year. Certain flies hatch and swarm early in the season, but others do so in late summer and autumn. Examples of the former are the large "drakes" (e.g. *Ephemera danica*) which flyfishermen usually call "Mayflies": they hatch during an intensive period between May and June, and capture the interest of trout. Among the later appearing flies are many species of caddis (sedge) fly, which often dominate northern waters from early summer until well into the autumn.

Selecting the fly

Trout eagerly focus upon the insects that are predominant during a given period. Thus, a flyfisherman has to adapt his or her choice of flies accordingly – a task made easier with a basic knowledge of entomology. True, one can determine the right fly in most cases by simply observing which insects seem to be most active. But the main fly on a particular day, for instance, has an underwater stage; and if one does not know how it looks, one cannot change from a dry fly to a wet imitation of the right colour, size and type, if the trout eventually stops taking the winged insect on the surface and becomes obsessed with the underwater form, nymphs or pupae, which are rising to hatch. Awareness of the commonest insects and their different life forms is, therefore, the key to good and interesting flyfishing.

Stages of growth

Most flies on flowing waters have undergone a long process of underwater life before they hatch into winged, sexually mature insects. These winged insects are just a reproductive stage, which is important in several ways for the survival of their species. The flies travel upstream to lay their eggs, compensating for the downstream drift that is constantly affecting eggs, larvae, nymphs or pupae. If the flies were to mate underwater, the whole population would shift during a few genera-

tions out to the mouth of the stream or river in a large lake or sea – and the waterway would then be emptied of insects. Any insects that reached the sea and its salty water would be unadapted to this environment, and the population would die out.

Current-living flies are, of course, very small and delicate creatures, unable to resist the violent force of flowing water. Since they must drift downstream continually, they have developed a final winged mating stage. It allows them to compensate for the drift by flying back upstream after mating, in order to lay their eggs. In this way, they manage to stay in suitable biotopes and ensure the survival of their species.

The nymph

After mating, the flies lay eggs in the water, where these develop into small larvae. The following cycle of development differs according to the specie of fly. Some species undergo an "incomplete metamorphosis", meaning that their larvae become ever bigger and turn into nymphs. A nymph resembles the adult fly in body form and character, except that it has no wings, although wing rudiments are clearly visible on the back of its breast segment. Flies with a nymph stage include the mayflies which are so important to flyfishermen. Further examples of this kind are stoneflies and damselflies.

After shedding their skin several times – much as an ordinary crustacean changes its shell – the nymphs are fully grown and rise to the surface, where they hatch. The nymph's skin cracks along its back and the winged, mature mayfly creeps out, destined to swarm and mate. Throughout its life as an egg, larva and nymph, the insect has been drifting downstream; yet when the fertilized females fly upstream to lay eggs, the cycle is completed.

The pupa

Other flies experience a "complete metamorphosis". Instead of becoming nymphs, they go through a pupal stage, during which the larvae are transformed into winged insects. In this case, there is no real similarity between the larva and the adult insect. Flies that hatch as pupae include the caddis flies, a group of great importance as models for our fishing flies. Midges are also an instance of this kind.

In sum, the life cycle of a caddis fly or a midge consists of an egg, a larva, a pupa, and a mature winged fly which – like the mayfly – travels upstream in order to lay eggs after mating.

Recognizing species

With time, the fisherman can easily get to know some species, such as the mayflies, and learn how their different nymphs look. For these species are not very abundant, and they have distinctive appearances. But when it comes to caddis flies and midges, there are difficulties.

The species of caddis fly are much more numerous than those of mayflies. In addition, it is often impossible to determine the species of caddis flies without a microscopic investigation of their sexual organs. Likewise, for example in Scandinavia alone, no fewer than five hundred species of midges are believed to exist. A fly-fisherman, therefore, can hardly be expected to keep them all in mind – nor is this necessary.

Group characteristics

To choose the right imitation, it is enough to know the sizes, colours and forms of the particular species that occur in one's own fishing waters. The essential point is to recognize, not individual insects, but the groups they belong to, whether each of these has a nymph or a pupal stage, and what it looks like. This can be done by studying the stomach contents of fish that are caught, or by using a drift-net to catch insects in the fishing waters. One then discovers that the similarities within each insect group are considerable. And at the same time, one acquires the experience of colour and size differences which is needed for selecting the right fly on a given day.

Flowing waters

Another lesson is that insects have body characteristics which do not simply depend on hereditary membership in a certain family, but can be common

Numerous species of mayflies inhabit flowing waters. A common variety is the "spinner" (Heptagenia), illustrated twice here: (above right) a recently hatched

to many groups and are due to the environment they live in. As a result, insects differ greatly according to whether they inhabit flowing or still waters, because the latter contrast in living conditions. Nevertheless, even in flowing waters we may find each species occupying a separate area, or indeed a separate "niche" in that area with very peculiar environmental requirements. While the variations in appearance between such insects may, at first, seem insignificant for our attempts to imitate them with fishing flies, it can be worth paying attention to the variations, as well as to the right technique for presenting a specific fly.

Strong current

Species that need plenty of oxygen live in areas of relatively strong current. But to survive in these areas, they must adapt both their appearance and their behavior. Consequently, such a nymph creeps on powerful, clawed legs. It has a flat body which minimizes its resistance to the water and, in fact, makes the water press it securely onto solid surfaces. Often we find the nymphs attached to the undersides of stones on the bottom of the water.

Insects vary in their environmental requirements. Some species of mayfly, such as spinners, need plenty of oxygen and thus occur mainly in fast-flowing waters. The nymphs are particularly well-suited to these surroundings.

Good illustrations are the mayfly nymphs in species of *Heptagenia*, such as *H. sulphurea* – "The Yellow May". There nymphs are difficult for a trout to catch, except when they release their grip and drift downstream to colonize new areas. This happens when a part of the stream bottom becomes too densely populated with nymphs, forcing them to spread into places with more food.

Such a drift also occurs when the nymphs are hatching. They are then seen higher up in the water, as the nymphs must reach the surface in order to become winged flies. Naturally, trout in the vicinity are not slow to seize the opportunity of taxing their numbers.

Here again, we notice how valuable it is for a flyfisherman to have a basic knowledge of entomology. If one knows the appearance of a Yellow May nymph, one can choose the right nymph imitation even if, at the time, no nymphs are visible, but only the sulphuryellow flies at the surface.

Weak current

Calmer sections of the same waterway are a home for other mayfly nymphs. These have more rounded bodies and less powerful legs. Due to the lower current speed, which mixes less oxygen into the water, they have usually developed larger and more lobe-shaped gills on the backs of their bodies, so as to increase their oxygen intake.

Examples of such nymphs are found in species of *Leptophlebia* – the adults popularly called "claret spinners" or "sepia spinners". They need not grip the bottom very hard, and can often be seen among the plants higher up – unless they are swimming about

In calm currents, it is not unusual for trout to stand with their heads toward the bottom when looking for food. In shallow water, one can sometimes even see their tail fins protruding from the surface.

Lakes and other still waters are also habitats for fish that have adapted to life in them. Here we find species that seldom or never occur in flowing waters. These fish can more easily feed on insects during their entire life cycle. And with the help of a float-ring, the fisherman finds it easier to reach the fish...

freely for short distances. Obviously, flies with this sort of behaviour and environment are much easier for trout to catch.

For flyfishermen, it is once more a matter of learning to recognize the nymphs, and to fish with well-tied imitations of some stage in their life cycle that occurs in the open water – either freely swimming, drifting, or rising to the surface in order to hatch.

Taken on the rise

Similarly, certain kinds of caddis-fly larvae have adapted to different water environments. Free-living larvae stay down among the bottom stones, and are frequently inaccessible to trout. They can be taken only when drifting with the current to places downstream.

Other species of caddis-fly larvae, known as "case-

worms", protect themselves with a body-cover built of various materials. Despite this artifice, they commonly creep around on the bottom and become easy prey for trout – which are glad to gobble both them and their cases.

Most caddis-fly larvae, though, are adequately protected by their way of life. Thus it is mainly after the pupal stage is finished that they are taken by trout, just as they head for the surface to hatch. Such hatches of pupae can be extremely massive, and are real peaks of excitement during the fishing year.

Still waters

Unlike the situation in flowing waters, where trout can seldom catch insect larvae, nymphs, or pupae until these drift or hatch, still waters offer constant opportunities. Species here are normally more accessible throughout their life cycles, since many live among the plants in free water.

Besides, further species occur which are not found in flowing waters. Some species are so tolerant that they can thrive in both calm and gently moving waters. Among these are midges and certain damselflies, which at times are very important to the flyfisherman. Already at the start of the season, for instance, the damselfly nymphs are quite large, while many mayfly nymphs need additional growth. The midges give birth to several generations during the whole summer, and these provide the fundamental food for fish in numerous waters.

Diurnal migrations

Whereas flowing water is seldom deep enough to prevent sunlight from reaching the bottom, conditions are different in a lake. The light does not penetrate to a lake bottom so easily. Hence only shallow areas out in the lake, as well as the shore zone, are productive enough to maintain sizeable insect populations.

In contrast to flowing waters, a lake does not enable the insects to drift. But they can undertake migrations back and forth along the shore zone, when the light fades in the evening or brightens in the morning. They are followed by fish and, as every lake flyfisherman has experienced, the fish come closer to land with the gathering dusk.

Lakes do, however, display an interesting type of drift. It occurs when the wind creates bands or lee edges on the water surface, for example in a cove which is exposed to the wind with its back to lee. In these edges is concentrated a drift of insects that are hatching, or have been blown out from land. Such a passage often provides good fishing places in still water.

The rewards of understanding

Lake insects also make their final trip up to the surface to hatch; and just as in flowing waters, this makes the trout focus upon the unprotected insects near the surface, when they are at a highly vulnerable phase of their development. It is now that the flyfisherman speaks of a "rise". With the right knowledge of the different kinds of insects, one can have unforgettable fishing experiences on these occasions.

All of the above situations show that entomology gives us basic facts that increase our understanding of how to fish with flies, and how to choose the best insect imitations in different types of water at various times of the fishing season. Beyond this, each of us may choose to study individual insects in greater detail, and thus get more out of the sport.

Next we shall take a closer look at some of the insects and other small water-living animals which are eaten by trout, and which are therefore leading models for artificial flies.

Mayflies

Although mayflies are not the dominant insect group in most waters, they have been a general symbol for flyfishing ever since the early days of the sport in England. It was also primarily mayflies that supplied the models for the first artificial imitation flies. This is because the "cradle" of flyfishing lay on the English chalk streams, where living conditions were notably good for mayflies. Many a fly pattern was born there and spread across the world – even to regions in which other insects rule the water fauna.

Mayflies belong to the order Ephemeroptera. Its name refers to the mayfly's short life as a winged insect, but actually a mayfly is not very short-lived. It spends most of its existence underwater as a larva and nymph, and its life cycle is as follows.

Mayflies have always been of interest to the flyfisherman, even though their importance has decreased with time - partly since a mayfly spends most of its life as a larva or nymph. This kind of insect undergoes an incomplete metamorphosis: it lays eggs that hatch into larvae, which grow into nymphs without going through a pupal stage. The nymphs swim to the surface and turn into winged duns, which moult their skins to become sexually mature spinners. In this final stage, the insects swarm and the females lay eggs, then die as "spent spinners".

Development and moulting

Once hatched from eggs, the small larvae grow into a nymph stage, with a body form like the winged fly's. As it develops, the nymph repeatedly outgrows and moults its skin. Each time, it becomes relatively pale with a soft new skin, so it lies inactive under a stone or other shelter until the new skin has hardened. Then it regains its darker colour as well – a transition that can profitably be studied in an insect aquarium.

With each moulting, too, the nymph is a little larger, and the wing-cases on the back of its breast segment (thorax) develop increasingly. The wings lie folded together like a parachute in a bag. When the time for hatching approaches, the nymph become ever more restless, and one day it suddenly rises to the surface. The skin crack along the back between the wing-cases, and out crawls the mayfly.

But the young mayfly is not yet complete. Upon emerging, it has a dull colour, half-transparent wings, and rather short tails. In flyfishing jargon, it is then called a *dun*. Soon it flies up and settles on the vegeta-tion at the shore edge. There it undergoes a further change of skin, and the sexually mature fly – a *spinner* – creeps out. This has a more brilliant body colour and shimmering, transparent wings.

The tails have also become longer, which is important since they help the fly to balance when it falls down through the swarm during its mating dance. In addition, one can now see a clear difference between males and females. A male has bigger eyes; its front legs and tails are longer; and its abdomen are two small claws, with which it grips the female as they mate.

Diverse life cycles

A swarming takes place over the waterway or the shore vegetation. Large swarms fly upward, then let themselves fall through a whole cloud of mayflies. At the

Two mayflies and three artificial flies. The latter resemble their natural prototypes closely enough to whet the appetites of trout.

Different stages in the mayfly's life cycle which are of value to flyfishermen - and some imitations of them.
After a mating dance, the spent spinners fall dead onto the water surface, and drift with the current - until taken, perhaps, by trout.

Just before hatching into the winged mayfly, a nymph has swum up to the surface. It lies there unprotected while its skin cracks between the wing sacs. Such an emerger is an easy and attractive prey for trout. Likewise, with an imitation of it on the leader, trout can readily be caught.

When the winged dun first emerges from its nymphal skin, it is not yet fully developed. Compared to the mature spinner, it has short tail antennae and only partly transparent wings, as well as a duller colour.

In the nymph stage, a mayfly grows continually and has to change its skin at regular intervals. A nymph that has recently moulted is often rather pale in colour, but soon regains its darker hue. As long as it stays on the bottom, it is hard for trout to get at. But once it approaches the surface to hatch, its role as fish food may well be fulfilled.

beginning, only males are usually visible – but shortly afterward, the females arrive and participate in the mating dance. Each female is soon gripped by a male and, once fertilized, she flies upstream to lay her eggs, a new generation.

Some species, such as the large *Ephemera danica* and *vulgata*, have a long life cycle in which they can remain nymphs for up to two years. I myself have observed the former to avoid hatching in a year with poor weather conditions, and to hatch massively in the following year when the weather improved. Thus two generations hatched at the same time, and the nymphs which had waited for a year were definitely the bigger.

Most mayfly species, though, have a year-long life cycle. Some others produce two generations every year, hatching in both spring and autumn. This is possible because the insects – just like the trout – are cold-blooded. Their development is delayed if the water is cold, and they grow only when it gets warmer. Certain species even spend the winter as eggs, and do not hatch into larvae until the sun begins to warm the water next spring.

Useful models

From a fishing standpoint, the mayfly's eggs and larvae are of no interest. The same applies to nymphs in those species that lie buried at the bottom of the water, like the above-mentioned *Ephemera danica* and *vulgata* as well as some small *Caenis* species. It can also be said of the species whose nymphs creep around beneath the bottom stones, such as *Heptagenia sulphurea*. Only when they drift with the water to colonize new bottom areas, or when they approach the surface to hatch, are the trout able to eat them in significant quantities. Nor is there any reason to tie imitations of light-coloured nymph variants which have recently moulted their skin, since they stay in hiding and cannot be adequately presented.

Instead, one must focus on drifting or hatching nymphs, and on the mayfly's winged dun or spinner stages. Moreover, one should have imitations of the kinds of nymphs which live among the water plants or swim freely in the water.

Distinct appearances

As we have seen, mayfly nymphs vary in size and body form according to their species. Along the abdomen are gills, which also differ in appearance with the species' environment and demands on water quality. Yet a common feature is the relatively elongated rear body itself. Another is the marked thorax section, with wing cases that become ever larger as a nymph grows closer to hatching. Further, all mayfly nymphs have three tails, regardless of how many tails the adult mayfly will possess.

The winged mayflies exhibit their own differences in colour and size. Their dun and spinner stages are distinguishable too. As if that were not enough, the sexes usually contrast in colour. Males always have longer tails and larger eyes than do females. Some adults have three tails, but there are species with just two.

A mayfly has two pairs of wings – in other words, four wings. However, only the front pair is fully developed and constantly held upright. This is the mayfly's hallmark, compared with other flies of interest to fly-fishermen. The rear pair of wings is retarded in its development; on some species, they are hardly a fourth as big as the front pair, and in others they amount to small rudiments.

Stoneflies

Like mayflies, the stoneflies undergo an incomplete metamorphosis, passing through a nymph stage which resembles the adult fly except that it lacks wings. But apart from some localities, the stoneflies have not been considered as important for fishing as mayflies. The reason is that, due to their life among the bottom stones, they are no easier for a trout to catch than the creeping mayfly nymphs are; and in terms of fishing technique, they are very hard to present in a suitable manner. Certainly they are eaten while drifting – yet their hatching also makes them less interesting than most other insects on the trout's menu. As a rule, stonefly nymphs creep up along a water plant or stone in order to hatch. Although a few hatch freely, riding on the water with raised wings, and can be mistaken for mayflies at a distance, the wings are laid down over the back as soon as they dry.

Like mayflies, the stonefly undergoes incomplete metamorphosis. Flyfishermen can use imitations of winged stoneflies to good advantage, notably in early spring, but their greatest interest is in the nymphs. Shown at left are the natural prototypes and imitations of the winged insect and nymph.

Early hatching

Many stoneflies hatch early in the spring, when the insects on the water are not numerous. A smart flyfisherman keeps some stonefly imitations in his box for such occasions. Even in cold northerly waters with a limited insect fauna, the stoneflies – especially their nymphs – may periodically have a great impact on the fishing.

Stoneflies and their nymphs are usually dark brown or nearly black. Both the nymphs and adults possess flat bodies, double wing-cases or wings, two tails on the body's last segment, and antennae on the head. Thus, the only real difference is that the nymphs are wingless. An adult's four wings, in two pairs, lie flat over the body – unlike a mayfly's wings, which stand upright. At a glance, stoneflies might seem to resemble another insect group, the caddis flies. But the latter hold their four wings obliquely over the abdomen, so that the upper wing edges meet in a ridge recalling a house roof.

Damselflies

One more group of insects with incomplete metamorphosis are the dragonflies. Among their subgroups, the nymphs of damselflies are most important for fishing in still waters, although some species occur in slowly flowing waters.

Damselfly nymphs are relatively large already at the start of the season. Imitations of them are therefore valuable when flyfishing in lakes and other calm waters throughout the season. They have a long, slim abdomen, three big wide tails (which actually are gills), and an elongated thorax section whose wing cases lie parallel to the body on its back. The nymphs

Damselflies are a sub-order of dragonflies, and thus undergo incomplete metamorphosis. Especially as nymphs, they are very important to flyfishermen in lakes and other still waters. The nymphs are characterized by a long, slim body and by three bladelike posterior gills. Imitations are often tied with marabou fibres, to be fished in a jerky manner.

Dragonflies are of little significance for flyfishing in their winged form, but the nymphs play a substantial role. Unlike those of damselflies, true dragonfly nymphs are short and thick. In many waters, they provide important food for fish and are an attractive prey, as they move in the mud or swim among the plants in lakes and ponds.

climb about on plants, down in the water, but they may also venture on short swim-tours with wiggling movements of their body and gill-leaves.

Modelling the nymphs

That damselflies are relatives of the true dragonflies is evident from the winged adults' appearance. But the alert flyfisherman will notice an essential difference: when at rest, a dragonfly holds its wings fully out-stretched to the sides, whereas damselflies close their wings flatly against each other atop the back.

Adult damselflies, though, play only a small role as models for fishing flies. What interest us are the nymphs. Since they inhabit the belts of underwater plants in lakes, their colour is normally green or green-ish brown. While their appearance is easy to imitate on the hook, it is equally important to copy their swim-ming technique by bringing them in with short pulls on the line. This wiggling movement is aided by the choice of tying materials; soft, lively marabou fibres have become very popular when imitating damselfly nymphs. Presentation of their way of swimming is see-mingly as attractive to the fish as an exact imitation.

Caddis flies

Originally, mayflies were the insect group which, in England, provided the models for most fishing flies. Yet elsewhere in the world, caddis-fly imitations have gained in significance because, on many waters, these are the dominant insects.

In contrast to mayflies, stoneflies and damselflies, a life cycle with complete metamorphosis is undergone by caddis flies, meaning that they have a pupal stage. The eggs are hatched into larvae, which look and develop differently according to their species. Some are free-living, such as *Rhyacophila*, whose clear-green larvae creep among the bottom stones in flowing waters.

Other caddis flies spin diverse kinds of nets, with which they filter the water for food. Among these are *Hydropsyche*, the "water spirits", a quite widespread species of caddis fly, and thus important as an imita-tion for the flyfisherman. Its larva is light beige in colour, with a dark brown forebody. The well-known Gold Ribbed Hare's Ear is an excellent imitation fly in numerous caddis-fly waters.

Species survival

Besides the free-living and net-spinning larvae of caddis flies, there are species which build a "house" or case from small grains of gravel, pieces of water plants or other bottom material. They carry these cases for protection, and pupate in them after closing the openings. If one finds such a case – apparently abandoned on the bottom – and opens it, one often finds a brown cocoon, through whose half-transparent wall the pupa can be seen. In the remaining species, the larva builds not a house, but a similar structure around itself, only when it undergoes metamorphosis.

During the pupal stage, the larva's body form becomes ever more like the adult caddis fly's. Its legs and antennae grow out, and two wing pairs develop to lie along the pupa's sides. When the time comes for hatching, the pupa leaves its sheltered cocoon and rises to the water surface, where it turns into a winged caddis fly. Since the pupae and hatching flies are so vulnerable, nature has evolved massive hatching as a method for enabling sufficiently many pupae to get through this "obstacle course" and ensure that their species survive.

At the same time as massive hatching helps to protect the caddis-fly species, it creates a huge concentration in the surface water for a limited period, and thus a surplus of food for trout. During such a hatch, the trout gather to a feast that the flyfisherman may long remember.

Silvery effects

Caddis-fly pupae vary in size and colour with their species, but are commonly beige to light brown, often including a dash of olive-green, although some display yellow or brighter yellow. All have a relatively thick abdomen and a darker thorax section, the wings lying along the sides together with the folded antennae and

Knowledge of the trout's food - including the choice of flies and how to present them - is at least as valuable as concentration and patience, if one wants to become an adept trout flyfisherman.

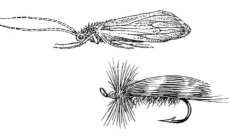

Caddis flies undergo a complete metamorphosis. In many parts of the world, they are the dominant insect group. Adults typically have wings laid like a roof on the back, long antennae, and usually a brown to greyish colour. Their imitations are best fished in a slithering manner on the water surface.

During its pupal stage, the caddis-fly larva becomes ever more similar to an adult. Finally it leaves the pupal "house", rises to the surface and hatches. On the way up, it is naturally easy for trout to take - which makes such hatches a great attraction for both the fish and the flyfisherman.

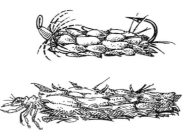

Some species of caddis fly have larvae that build "houses" or spin little nets. Others have free-living larvae, such as the species Rhyacopila. Its bright-green larvae are frequently seen creeping among the bottom stones in flowing waters.

What we call case-worms are caddis-fly larvae that build "houses" from bottom materials such as gravel and plant particles. They carry these houses for protection, until they close the openings and pupate. Houses that seem to be abandoned often contain both a cocoon and a pupa.

legs. One pair of legs is longer than the others; these "paddle-legs" resemble hairy oars, and help the pupa to swim in water or kick itself along the surface. The pupae are rather plump, and can be seen easily in the water when they swim toward the surface with their strong paddle-legs.

No less conspicuous is their technique for releasing themselves from their skin. They pump in air between the skin and body, which gives them a shimmering silver appearance. This effect is quite visible underwater, and many flyfishermen exploit it when composing pupa patterns. One can, for example, like the American fly-fisherman Gary LaFontaine, tie imitations with shiny Antron yarn in the form of a sac enclosing an air bubble – or, like his compatriot Pete Hidy, use a dubbed body containing lots of tiny air bubbles – so as to get a "mimicry" effect. Another method is to tie weighted

pupae with dubbed bodies, then grease them to produce the silvery look.

The layer of air gives the pupa more buoyancy, allowing it to reach the water surface faster and leave its skin. But this layer also has the disadvantage of helping trout to detect the pupa.

Varied habits

The pupae that succeed in reaching the surface hatch into caddis flies which, normally, have long antennae and are coloured grey-brown to brown, with four slightly hairy wings on their backs. These adults do not soar as elegantly as mayflies. Their somewhat heavy flight and flickering wing movements find a good imitation in a fairly well-dressed hackled dry fly. Often they travel densely over the water, and trout

A scene like this occurs when trout take caddis-fly pupae that are approaching the surface to hatch. Due to their splashing, the trout may seem to be taking food on the surface, but they are actually eating just beneath it. Thus, a dry-fly fisherman need not try to catch them.

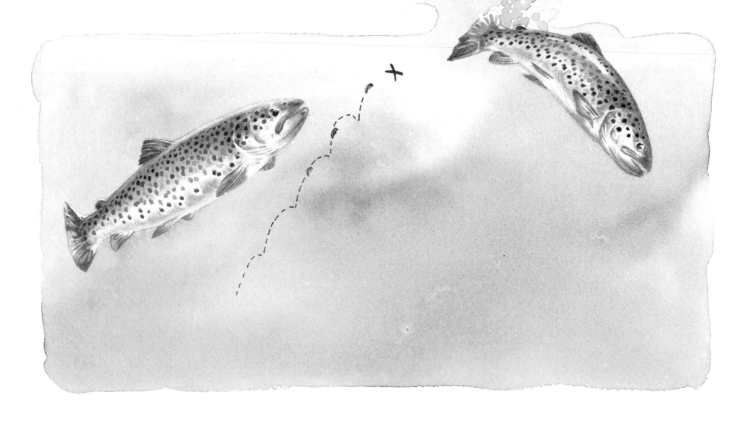

In certain species of caddis fly, the larvae surround themselves with "houses" made of gravel, sand and plants from the bottom. The houses' appearance and shape depend on the environment and current conditions. For example, the larvae in flowing waters build flatter houses than do those in lakes or other still waters, to lower the risk of being swept away by the current. House-building caddis-fly species adapt well to their surroundings, and can thus occur in diverse forms.

occasionally leap up to take them, though most interested in the easily caught pupae rising to the surface.

The pattern of hatching differs not only between species, but also according to the temperature and humidity. The warmer it is, the more smoothly and quickly the hatching proceeds. While some pupae seem to leave their skins already under the water and fly away as soon as they get to the surface, others may be seen paddling for long distances on the surface. The latter form "streaking" that is obvious to both the fish and the fisherman. This can be imitated by pulling an artificial fly rapidly along the surface.

The pupae are thus capable of much activity, and I have often watched certain species racing about on the water's surface tension, or on plants and stones in an insect aquarium. Such studies are extremely valuable sources of knowledge on how the insects move and behave, as well as on the varying appearances of insects and of related nymphs and pupae. For a fly imitation is not finished when it leaves the tying vise – one has to understand how to fish it, too.

The mating and egg-laying of caddis flies also show differences according to their species. Here the patterns are not as consistent as in mayflies. Caddis flies are frequently seen mating on trees and bushes far inland. The females may be taken by fish when they return to the water for egg-laying, but they are of less interest to a flyfisherman than the pupae.

Important imitations

Never the less all of the caddis fly's stages of development are among the leading models for insect imitations by fishermen in northern latitudes. Since it is less sensitive to pollution than mayflies often are, its importance has grown recently – in step with the acidification and poor quality of many waterways.

There are numerous successful caddis-fly imitations such as Européa 12, Rackelhanen, Elk Hair Caddis, and Streaking Caddis, to name only some which should not be absent from your fly-box. When comings to the larvae, fishing in flowing waters can occasionally benefit by, for example, drifting imitations of *Hydropsyche*, a good one being the Gold Ribbed Hare's Ear. Likewise, case-worms in the form of weighted, densely hackled, trimmed Palmer flies, tied on small streamer hooks, can be excellent lake flies – fished slowly with a sink-line down on the bottom.

Some well-known caddis-fly imitations:

Goddard's Caddis (winged insect)

Emergent Sparkle Pupa (pupa on its way to hatch)

Gold Ribbed Hare's Ear (free-living, drifting larva)

Gill-Ribbed larva (frilevande, driftande larv)

Borsten (case-worm)

Midges and gnats

Midges, as well as gnats (especially black-flies), being widespread and abundant during almost the whole season, are often the fish's staple diet. Both belong to the insect order *Diptera*, meaning two-winged; and they undergo complete metamorphosis, passing through a pupal stage. But the latter are difficult to imitate because of their size and way of life.

For instance, the gnat larvae are attached to objects in the water; even if very numerous, they are so tiny and immobile that they can hardly be copied by fishing flies. The pupa's house is also firmly anchored, and eventually the complete insect hatches from it. The gnat surrounds itself with an air-case, and – just like a caddis fly's pupa – has a shiny silver appearance when it rises to the water surface.

Different kinds of mosquitoes and gnats are something of a basic food for trout in many waters - largely because they are abundant during much of the fishing season. It is mainly the air-filled, silver-shiny pupae which interest fish and, therefore, fishermen. During the often massive hatches, trout tend to swim just below the water surface and feed at leisure. In spite of this, they may be hard to lure, even with the best-tied imitations.

Midges hatch primarily during windless mornings and evenings, when the water is smooth as a mirror. Since the trout tend to approach the shore under cover of darkness, one should fish from a position somewhat up on land, to avoid scaring them.

Stiff competition

Hatches of gnats are quite massive. The trout may then become entirely selective and concentrate on eating gnats. Despite their small size, such quantities mean that it does not take much energy to catch them. One can imitate hatching gnats with a simple fly whose body is made of peacock herl. This might be greased to create the shimmering silver layer of air around the fly. However, such artificial versions have to compete with the thousands of real, live gnats. So the fishing may prove frustrating, as the chances of a trout choosing one's fly during intensive hatches are minimal. The best chances are at the beginning or end of a hatch, when there are not as many gnats in or on the water.

Peculiar characteristics

Unlike the gnats, which develop only in rapid flowing waters, we find midges in still water and slowly moving pools. Among the speices of interest for the flyfisherman the male midge has feathery antennae and the females do not sting. There is a great number of subspecies, but since their life cycles coincide, we can regard them as a single group, including minor differences in colour and size.

Midge larvae have segmented bodies and resemble thin worms. They live on water plants, or buried in the bottom, until they pupate. Although a very important food of fish, these larvae are by no means easy to imitate with fishing flies. The main reason, of course, is that flies cannot be given an entomologically convincing presentation in the bottom material.

By contrast, the pupae are no problem for either imitation or presentation. They have a slender, segmented abdomen and a clearly marked thorax, with short wing-cases lying along the sides. On the midge's head these are pale, thread-like gills. When the pupae rise to the surface at hatching time, their bodies give the same shimmering silver impression that we have noticed in other kinds of insects. This, together with their body form and tufted gills, produces an appearance that can readily be imitated on a fly-hook.

The life cycle of midges is short, and some species give birth to several generations during a summer. Hence, they occur on the water all through the fishing season, and are one of the leading insect groups in most lakes and ponds. Midge pupae are also among the few that can make the fish select them exclusively when they hatch in large numbers.

Hanging in the surface

When hatching, a midge pupa is quite unprotected and hangs in the surface with its long rear body underwater. The speed of hatching depends on the air and water temperatures, but sometimes the pupa remains hanging for quite a while. In flyfishing literature, it is often described as if "lifeless". Yet I have observed, both in my insect aquaria and out on the water, that the pupa can show a fair amount of vitality, bending and wiggling its abdomen to free itself from the pupal skin.

As flyfishermen, therefore, we should focus upon this final stage of development into a winged midge, and allow our imitation to hang vertically in the surface film, giving it an occasional twitch with very short pulls on the line. Midge-pupa fishing can be exciting indeed. The fish swim right in the surface and graze calmly on the hatching pupae, with leisurely "head-and-tail" wakes that barely break the water.

These pupae vary in colour and size, but the majority range from green or brown to almost black. They are best imitated on No. 16-12 hooks. It is enough to tie a thin rear with silk far down on the hook bend, and a round dubbed ball for a thorax which, if greased, increases the buoyancy. A tuft of white poly yarn or marabou fibre can copy the gills on the head. One might add a single turn of sparsely fibred hackle, suggesting the legs that struggle on the water's surface film, and further adding to the buoyancy.

A midge pupa has a slim segmented rear body, well-marked thorax and short wing-sacs. It is easy to imitate and present, but only the last stage - from pupa to winged insect - is of interest in flyfishing. The pupa then hangs just in the water surface film, unprotected and easy for trout to take. The fish simply pass beneath the pupae and pluck them down. Shown below are some imitations of midge pupae, which have proved good at luring trout onto the hook: from top to bottom are a Footballer nymph, a Bow-Tie Buzzer, and an Iron Blue flymph.

On blustery days it can be rewarding to use imitations of land insects, such as crane-flies, on your leader tip. Crane-fly fishing is sometimes very popular, not least in Irish lakes.

Crane-flies

Encountered now and then on fishing waters, the crane-flies resemble midges, but are much bigger. Due to their size, and rich occurrence for a period in high summer, they are of some interest to the fly-fisherman.

An adult crane-fly is a couple of centimetres long. It has two oblong wings, which can be imitated with two hackle points; the back wings are retarded, consisting of only two club-like rudiments. The six long legs exhibit clear joints.

While a flyfisherman seldom can base his fishing upon crane-fly imitations, there is every reason to keep a few in the box. They are suitably tied on a thin hook with an extended shank – or on an ordinary hook, but in that case with a "detached" body. For the legs, strands from a pheasant-cock tail feather are used. To copy the knee joints, knots may be added on the legs before tying them on the body.

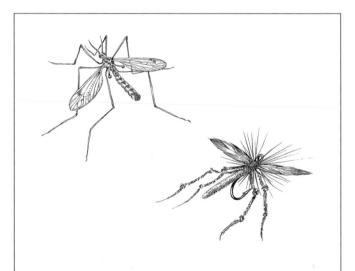

In strong wind, crane-flies are commonly blown out from land onto the water, where trout gladly take them at the surface. There are several imitations of crane-flies, perhaps the best-known being Daddy Long-Legs (above).
Crane-fly imitations are usually tied on a thin strea-mer hook. The legs may be made of strands from a pheasant cock's tail feather. To imitate the typical knee-joints, knots are added to the legs before tying them in.

Water boatmen and other bugs

The diet of trout also includes a host of "true bugs" – both species that live on land but are blown onto the water, and those that spend their whole lives underwater. The former are imitated with floating flies, to be fished on the surface, while the latter's imitations are weighted or tied with water-absorbent material that makes them sink. To the second group belong various sorts of diving bugs, as well as water boatmen, which are rather common in many still waters.

It is needless to know the species names and life cycles of water bugs, but one must study their appearances in order to imitate them properly. They often have a yellow-brown underside, and a shiny back-shield that ranges from dark brown to blue-black.

Characteristic, too, is their way of swimming up to the surface for taking in air, which gives them a silvery air-case, sometimes only a bubble at the tip of the rear body. This is imitated by placing a silver tag in the hook bend of the fly. Certain underwater bugs, such as water boatmen, also have long hairy paddle-legs, worth adding to the fly.

Snails and leeches

Other underwater fish food is provided by snails and leeches. Some fish are experts at consuming snails, and therefore specialize in them. However, these creatures are naturally hard to imitate, and to fish, realistically. Leeches are far more rewarding for both the flytier

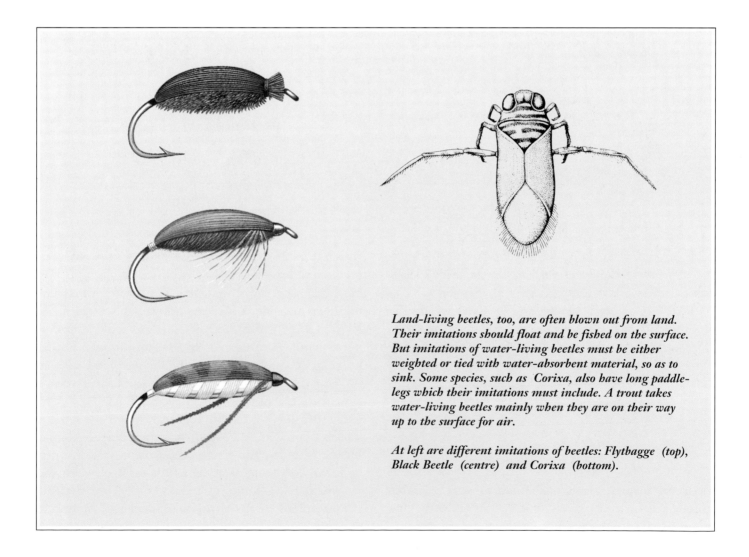

Land-living beetles, too, are often blown out from land. Their imitations should float and be fished on the surface. But imitations of water-living beetles must be either weighted or tied with water-absorbent material, so as to sink. Some species, such as Corixa, also have long paddle-legs which their imitations must include. A trout takes water-living beetles mainly when they are on their way up to the surface for air.

At left are different imitations of beetles: Flytbagge (top), Black Beetle (centre) and Corixa (bottom).

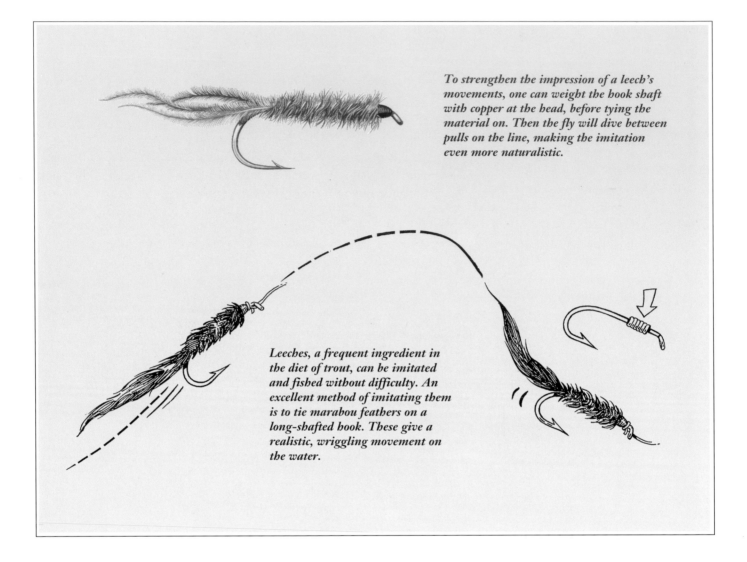

To strengthen the impression of a leech's movements, one can weight the hook shaft with copper at the head, before tying the material on. Then the fly will dive between pulls on the line, making the imitation even more naturalistic.

Leeches, a frequent ingredient in the diet of trout, can be imitated and fished without difficulty. An excellent method of imitating them is to tie marabou feathers on a long-shafted hook. These give a realistic, wriggling movement on the water.

and the fisherman. Long-tailed marabou flies acquire a lively gait in the water that copies the leech's slithering movements in a simple, striking manner.

To emphasize such movements, one can weight the front part of the hook shank before tying in the materials. The complete imitation will then have a diving gait through the water, straightening up when one pulls the line. This repetition makes the fly perform a leech's typical, twisting up and down way of swimming.

Crustaceans

In many waters, the trout obtain a very valuable supply of nutrition from diverse crustaceans. One example is *Gammarus*, a kind of small shrimp,

which does not easily tolerate acidic water environments and has thus widely declined or disappeared. Half-transparent, it has the peculiarity of swimming on its side. One can imitate it with a Gold Ribbed Hare's Ear tied on a hook with a humpbent shank. A more realistic version would have a beige-grey, dubbed body, which is wrapped with an olive or ginger-coloured Palmer hackle, tying down a back-shield of transparent polythene – after the hackle on the top is cut to barely protrude as legs under the shrimp, and as a few bristling antennae on the head. For the mating season in midsummer, gammarid shrimps become bright orange, so it can be worth tying some imitations of this variant too, if you intend to flyfish in gammarid-rich waters at the time.

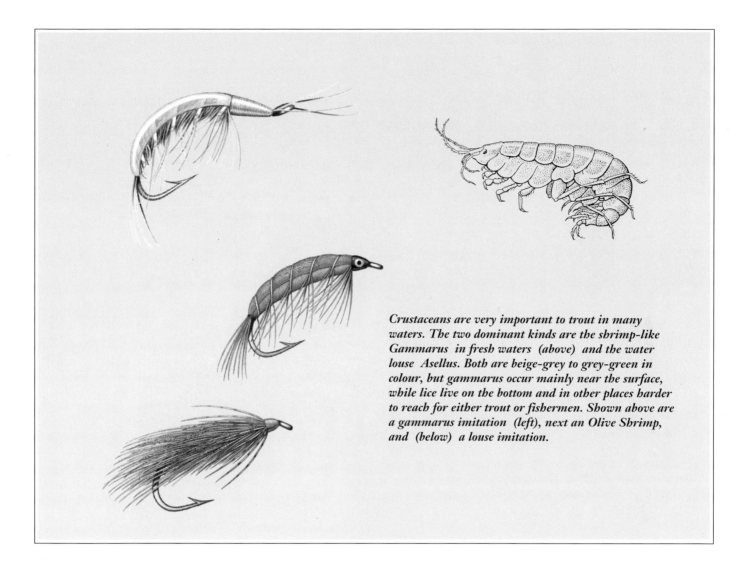

Crustaceans are very important to trout in many waters. The two dominant kinds are the shrimp-like Gammarus in fresh waters (above) and the water louse Asellus. Both are beige-grey to grey-green in colour, but gammarus occur mainly near the surface, while lice live on the bottom and in other places harder to reach for either trout or fishermen. Shown above are a gammarus imitation (left), next an Olive Shrimp, and (below) a louse imitation.

Fishing on the bottom

A further instance is *Asellus*, a type of water louse. More tolerant of acidification, it has kept up with this trend by proliferating in many lakes, where it takes over niches that other, more sensitive bottom-living animals and insects have been forced to abandon. It may reach large concentrations locally and, in some waters, has become the main food of fish during much of the year.

These lice, too, have a beige-grey to grey-green body colour. But unlike the side-compressed gammarids, they are compressed from on top. Their legs and long antennae project forward and to the sides of the flat, jointed body.

Water lice can also be imitated in detail. Yet here again, it usually suffices to use a weighted Gold Ribbed Hare's Ear, possibly trimmed above and below, with some straggling fibres pushed out to the sides as legs. A variant is to brush the fly with a toothbrush before trimming it, so that the fibres point slightly backward.

The problem with *Asellus* fishing is that – in contrast to fishing with *Gammarus* imitations just under the surface – water lice inhabit the bottom or the decaying parts of plants, where it is difficult to present a fly without snagging the hook. Still, after a flyfisherman has caught a trout whose stomach is stuffed with *Asellus*, will realize how important the louse can be as trout food in certain waters.

Land insects

During short but intensive periods, many land insects contribute significantly to the diet of trout. Moreover, for a few days – or sometimes only a few hours – they may occur in amounts so huge that the fish become wholly selective of the particular insects which are involved. These insects, while normally living inland, are blown over the water at occasions such as swarming, and fall abundantly onto the surface. Among them are the sloe bugs (stinkbugs) which appear on the reeds in lakes during the summer. Great numbers tumble into the water and are eaten by fish that may specialize on them for a short period.

Ants

Even more important are flying ants, which blow onto the water at various times in the summer when they swarm. Tiny they may be, yet the trout adore them – and being quite plentiful, they whet the fish's appetite until it seems to ignore all other insects, focusing on

Sloe bugs (stinkflies) are among the land insects that, when swarming, may blow out and fall onto the water. For short periods, the fish can become entirely devoted to these little beetles.

the winged ants as they hit the surface and are caught by its film.

Thus, flying ants should not be missing from your fly-box. As luck has it, they are very easy and rewarding to imitate. The ant has a segmented body with a marked waist that produces a characteristic silhouette. So the fly can consist of two dubbed sections made from small balls, separated by a few turns of soft hen hackle. The hackle need not be stiff because the ant lies low in the surface film. It is the dubbed body that provides buoyancy, while the hackle recreates only the ant's struggling legs.

Grasshoppers

On waters surrounded by grass, quantities of grasshoppers occur during the late summer and early autumn. These are relatively big insects and offer the trout an ample mouthful, so they are gratefully gobbled if they fall onto the water.

Consequently, at some places, grasshopper fishing has developed into its own discipline with many well-known fly patterns. The latter all have a fairly large, thick body with good buoyancy, and possibly wings laid flat over the body, as well as the characteristic long legs that stretch obliquely backward along the fly's sides.

Such fishing has been highly refined in the United States. In Scandinavia, for example, it is of recent origin, but some fine grasshopper waters exist – and there is even a small specie called a "water grasshopper", which appears only near water.

Besides the true insects, always six-legged, we find diverse spiders living near the water – and actually upon or within water. Terrestrial spiders may climb into a tree and spin a long, thin thread that carries them with the wind to new areas. Sometimes the flight ends over a lake, which does not generate such strong upwinds since it is warmed less than the adjacent land. This is a journey that can end in the jaws of a trout.

Small fish

An account of the insects and other animals that trout prey upon, and of their important roles as models for fishing flies, would be incomplete without mentioning imitations of small fish, including fry. The truth is that

Land insects, so-called terrestrials, occasionally provide trout with a large part of their nutrition. For example, when grasshoppers (above right) or flying ants (below right) fall onto the water in large quantities, the fish are often quite selective and may be difficult to catch with traditional fly patterns. Some imitations of land insects should thus be in your fly-box. At left, the illustration shows (from top) Balsageting, a yarn ant, a sloe bug, and a grasshopper (Henry's Fork Hopper).

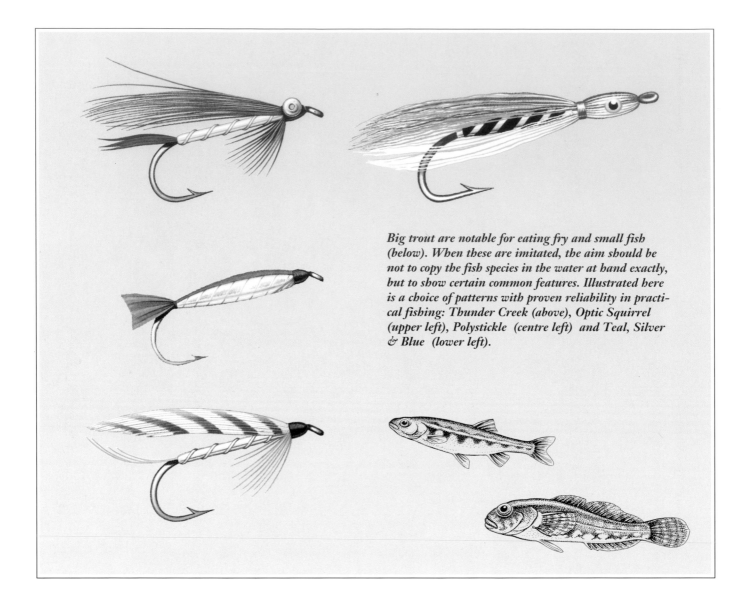

Big trout are notable for eating fry and small fish (below). When these are imitated, the aim should be not to copy the fish species in the water at hand exactly, but to show certain common features. Illustrated here is a choice of patterns with proven reliability in practical fishing: Thunder Creek (above), Optic Squirrel (upper left), Polystickle (centre left) and Teal, Silver & Blue (lower left).

only the trout which change to a diet of fish are able to break through the "growth barrier", meaning that they get the chance to become really big trout.

There are many kinds of small-fish imitations. They need not be detailed copies of the small fish that occur in a given body of water; some characteristics in common are enough. The body should be elongated, with a dark back and light belly. Marked, relatively large eyes seem to be the key stimulus that makes a trout interpret the fly as a small fish it can catch.

Among the better-known examples is the Thunder Creek series. Numerous other elongated streamer and bucktail flies can also yield fish. During recent years, more naturalistic imitations have appeared, with bodies

of braided mylar tubing that forms a fine scale pattern. The possibilities of variation are great, even within a few basic patterns. A flyfisherman is wise to find suitable colour combinations for his or her own fishing water, aided by stomach studies of the trout caught.

Cold-blooded creatures

Let us conclude where we began: with entomology as a reservoir of knowledge, not primarily about individual insects, but rather to increase our understanding of insects' living conditions and how these affect our flyfishing.

Like the trout, its prey are cold-blooded. All of them, not least the insects, experience rapid growth and activity when it is warm in the air and water, but live lethargically when it gets cold. For example, insects need a certain number of "day-degrees" in order to develop fully from egg to winged adult. Ten days at 3° C (37° F) in the water gives 30 day-degrees, but the same development occurs in five days if the average temperature is 6° C (43° F).

This explains such phenomena as the ability of some mayfly species to have a spring generation that lays eggs, which become complete flies already in the autumn, after a few months of warm water – whereas the autumn generation's eggs require a whole long autumn, winter and following spring to develop as far.

A fact ignored, unfortunately, by many trout flyfishermen is that trout are predatory fish. In particular, large trout are usually fish-eaters. Whoever wants to catch them should, therefore, fish with streamers and other fish imitations.

Environmental temperature

Whether they are larvae, nymphs, pupae, or winged flies, the daily activity of insects is proportional to the surrounding temperature. This is also true of trout, until their optimum temperature is reached, when they have the best nutrient intake and metabolism. If the temperature rises further, the water becomes less able to hold free oxygen, with negative effects on all water-living organisms. Thus, a cold-blooded animal reacts to the ambient heat in a quite different way than do humans and other warm-blooded beings, a fact that flyfishermen have good reason to keep in mind.

When the weather turns after a cold period, we can therefore expect greater activity on the water. More insects hatch and the trout respond to them. But the opposite happens if worse weather decreases the air and water temperatures. Even the hatched flies may then stay sitting in the bushes along a stream, and begin to swarm the very next evening if the air gets warmer and more comfortable again. The basic cause is their need to obtain energy from the environmental heat, in contrast to us who, through metabolism, can give ourselves the right body temperature. This is an important clue if we wonder at times why the fish are not taking.

The insect aquarium

Any flyfisherman interested in fishing on an entomological basis with imitation flies will profit by observing different water-living insects in an aquarium environment. Species that inhabit lakes can be preserved temporarily in a simple glass bottle with water from the lakes where they were collected.

Insects from flowing waters are harder to keep alive and require an aquarium with oxygenated current, but this is fairly easy to arrange. You can order a silicon-glued glass aquarium, measuring 30 x 60 cm at the bottom and 20 cm high, from a glazier's shop. Also buy a small submergible pump and place it in one corner of the aquarium. Half-fill the tank with water, making sure that the pump's outlet and inlet are in the water surface. Then build up an elongated island in the middle of the tank. The pump will create a current around this and, once

moving, the water's mass will spread the current around the whole tank. At the same time, the pump's surface location pulls in some air, which helps to oxygenate the water. Thus, current-living species that demand plenty of oxygen can be maintained in such an aquarium.

Continual learning

Aquarium studies have many advantages and yield experience of direct value, both in the tying stage and out on the fishing water. One can observe the actual appearances of various insects – such as the shimmering silver air-case that has been discussed above. This is a feature of pupae when they rise to the surface for hatching, yet is not seen if one catches a pupa by hand and lifts it out of the water. We can also learn insects' manifold patterns of movement, and get a better idea of how to fish each imitation.

Investigations on your own are not only informative, but will dramatically increase the pleasure of your hours spent on the water. To follow the insects' development, see how they pupate, and witness a fly hatch right in your living room, is a source of joy in itself as well.

Cold-blooded insects and animals obtain energy from the warmth of their surroundings. After a long cold period, for instance, the water warms up and the insects revive, enabling trout to eat more. Thus, changes in weather can be quite beneficial to the fish - no matter if the air and water are quickly warmed, or if an extended heat wave is broken by cooler weather.

Selected
fly patterns

While imitations of insects that live in and upon the water are an indispensable part of fly-fishing, and therefore provide models for our artificial imitations, many fantasy flies have also proved able to catch trout. These flies may not seem to resemble anything worth eating, but it is often the presentation and the fly's way of moving in the water that determine whether the fish will strike or not.

For example, the fantasy fly Red Palmer, with its soft hackle and seductive movements, can give a livelier impression of a small prey animal - even if its body is bright red - than a fly which is dressed in the correct colours but hangs stiff and dead on the leader. In other cases, the colour contrasts of a fly may attract fish to take it simply out of curiosity or aggressiveness.

Thus, our tradition of flying covers the whole range from exact insect imitations to pure fantasy flies.

Even if no insects can be seen on or near the water, it is possible to lure fish onto the hook. Whether or not the fish will take is often more dependent on how you present the fly, than on which fly pattern you choose. Still, of course, a well-filled fly-box should always accompany you to the water.

Wetflies

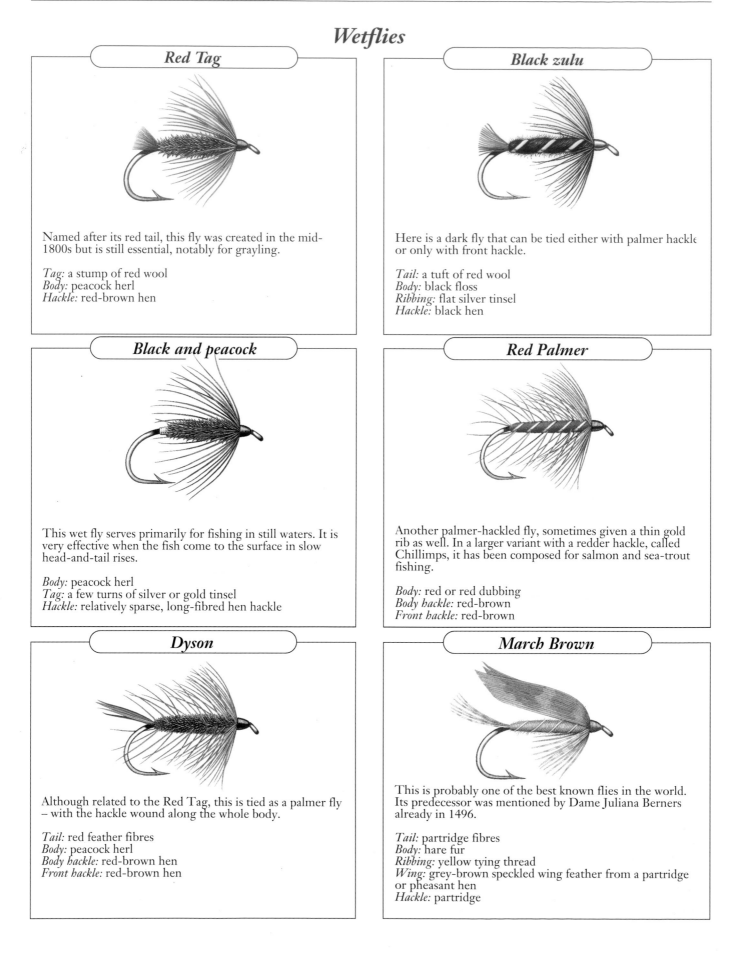

Red Tag

Named after its red tail, this fly was created in the mid-1800s but is still essential, notably for grayling.

Tag: a stump of red wool
Body: peacock herl
Hackle: red-brown hen

Black zulu

Here is a dark fly that can be tied either with palmer hackle or only with front hackle.

Tail: a tuft of red wool
Body: black floss
Ribbing: flat silver tinsel
Hackle: black hen

Black and peacock

This wet fly serves primarily for fishing in still waters. It is very effective when the fish come to the surface in slow head-and-tail rises.

Body: peacock herl
Tag: a few turns of silver or gold tinsel
Hackle: relatively sparse, long-fibred hen hackle

Red Palmer

Another palmer-hackled fly, sometimes given a thin gold rib as well. In a larger variant with a redder hackle, called Chillimps, it has been composed for salmon and sea-trout fishing.

Body: red or red dubbing
Body hackle: red-brown
Front hackle: red-brown

Dyson

Although related to the Red Tag, this is tied as a palmer fly – with the hackle wound along the whole body.

Tail: red feather fibres
Body: peacock herl
Body hackle: red-brown hen
Front hackle: red-brown hen

March Brown

This is probably one of the best known flies in the world. Its predecessor was mentioned by Dame Juliana Berners already in 1496.

Tail: partridge fibres
Body: hare fur
Ribbing: yellow tying thread
Wing: grey-brown speckled wing feather from a partridge or pheasant hen
Hackle: partridge

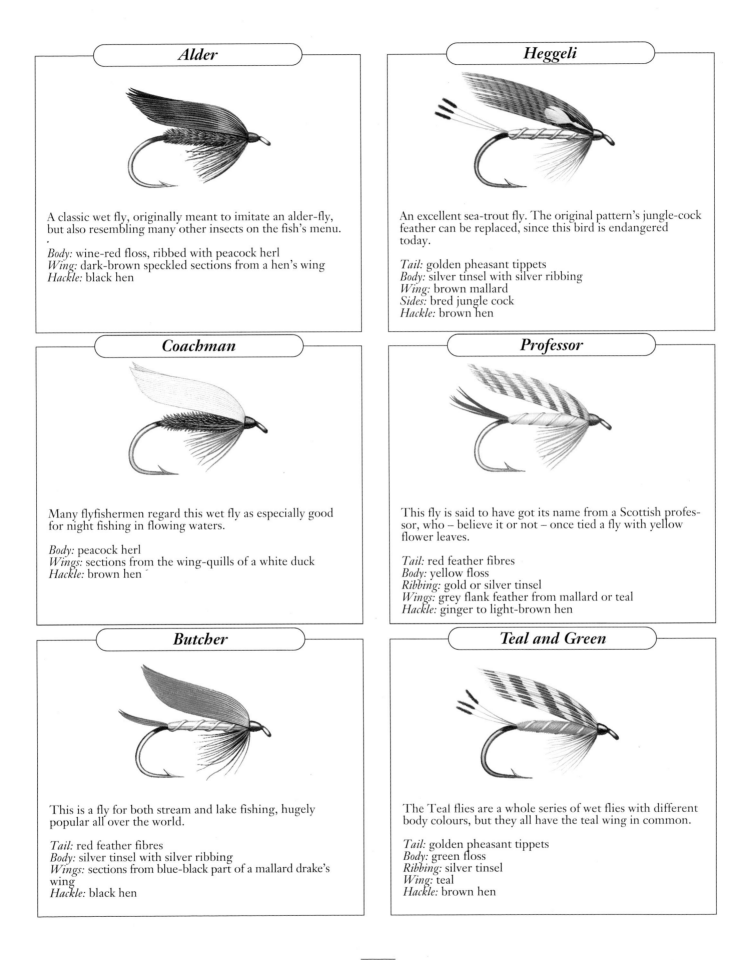

Alder

A classic wet fly, originally meant to imitate an alder-fly, but also resembling many other insects on the fish's menu.

Body: wine-red floss, ribbed with peacock herl
Wing: dark-brown speckled sections from a hen's wing
Hackle: black hen

Heggeli

An excellent sea-trout fly. The original pattern's jungle-cock feather can be replaced, since this bird is endangered today.

Tail: golden pheasant tippets
Body: silver tinsel with silver ribbing
Wing: brown mallard
Sides: bred jungle cock
Hackle: brown hen

Coachman

Many flyfishermen regard this wet fly as especially good for night fishing in flowing waters.

Body: peacock herl
Wings: sections from the wing-quills of a white duck
Hackle: brown hen

Professor

This fly is said to have got its name from a Scottish professor, who – believe it or not – once tied a fly with yellow flower leaves.

Tail: red feather fibres
Body: yellow floss
Ribbing: gold or silver tinsel
Wings: grey flank feather from mallard or teal
Hackle: ginger to light-brown hen

Butcher

This is a fly for both stream and lake fishing, hugely popular all over the world.

Tail: red feather fibres
Body: silver tinsel with silver ribbing
Wings: sections from blue-black part of a mallard drake's wing
Hackle: black hen

Teal and Green

The Teal flies are a whole series of wet flies with different body colours, but they all have the teal wing in common.

Tail: golden pheasant tippets
Body: green floss
Ribbing: silver tinsel
Wing: teal
Hackle: brown hen

Dry flies

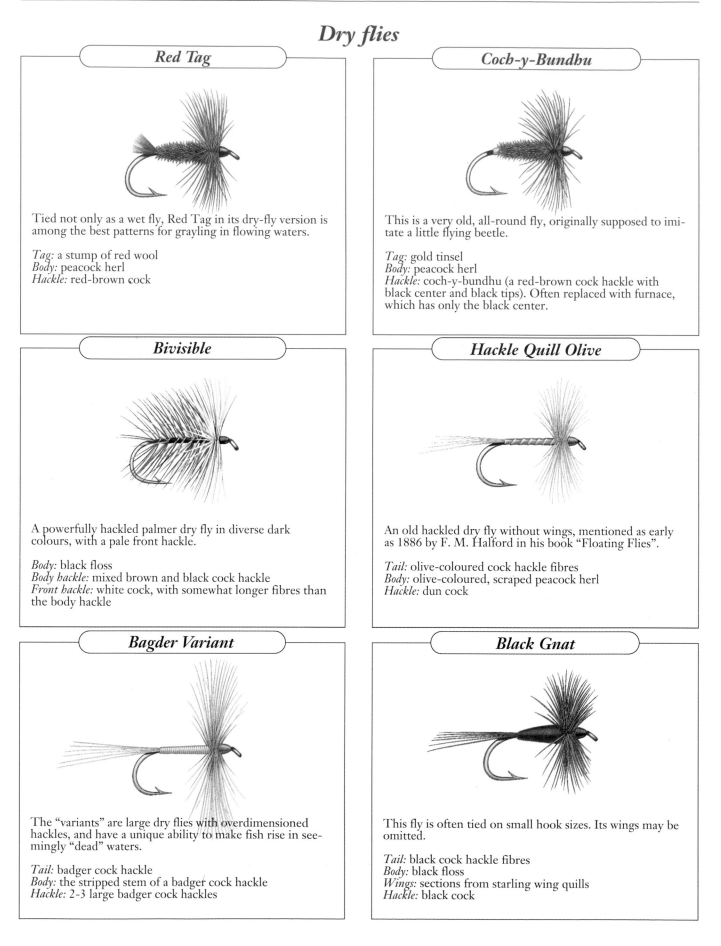

Red Tag

Tied not only as a wet fly, Red Tag in its dry-fly version is among the best patterns for grayling in flowing waters.

Tag: a stump of red wool
Body: peacock herl
Hackle: red-brown cock

Coch-y-Bundhu

This is a very old, all-round fly, originally supposed to imitate a little flying beetle.

Tag: gold tinsel
Body: peacock herl
Hackle: coch-y-bundhu (a red-brown cock hackle with black center and black tips). Often replaced with furnace, which has only the black center.

Bivisible

A powerfully hackled palmer dry fly in diverse dark colours, with a pale front hackle.

Body: black floss
Body hackle: mixed brown and black cock hackle
Front hackle: white cock, with somewhat longer fibres than the body hackle

Hackle Quill Olive

An old hackled dry fly without wings, mentioned as early as 1886 by F. M. Halford in his book "Floating Flies".

Tail: olive-coloured cock hackle fibres
Body: olive-coloured, scraped peacock herl
Hackle: dun cock

Bagder Variant

The "variants" are large dry flies with overdimensioned hackles, and have a unique ability to make fish rise in seemingly "dead" waters.

Tail: badger cock hackle
Body: the stripped stem of a badger cock hackle
Hackle: 2-3 large badger cock hackles

Black Gnat

This fly is often tied on small hook sizes. Its wings may be omitted.

Tail: black cock hackle fibres
Body: black floss
Wings: sections from starling wing quills
Hackle: black cock

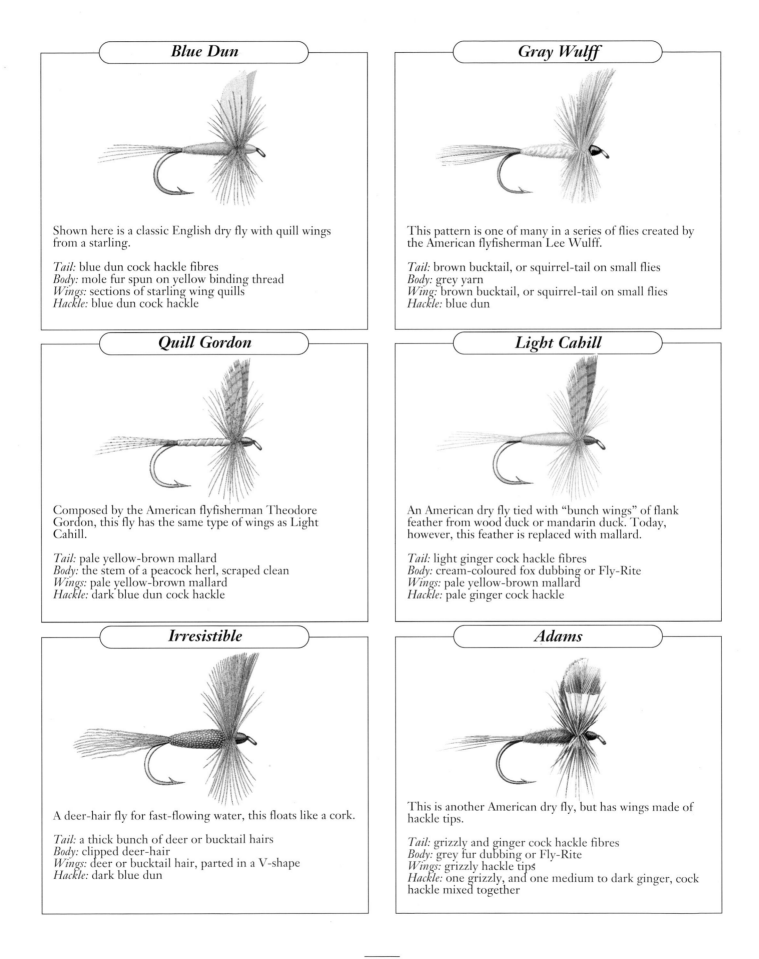

Blue Dun

Shown here is a classic English dry fly with quill wings from a starling.

Tail: blue dun cock hackle fibres
Body: mole fur spun on yellow binding thread
Wings: sections of starling wing quills
Hackle: blue dun cock hackle

Gray Wulff

This pattern is one of many in a series of flies created by the American flyfisherman Lee Wulff.

Tail: brown bucktail, or squirrel-tail on small flies
Body: grey yarn
Wing: brown bucktail, or squirrel-tail on small flies
Hackle: blue dun

Quill Gordon

Composed by the American flyfisherman Theodore Gordon, this fly has the same type of wings as Light Cahill.

Tail: pale yellow-brown mallard
Body: the stem of a peacock herl, scraped clean
Wings: pale yellow-brown mallard
Hackle: dark blue dun cock hackle

Light Cahill

An American dry fly tied with "bunch wings" of flank feather from wood duck or mandarin duck. Today, however, this feather is replaced with mallard.

Tail: light ginger cock hackle fibres
Body: cream-coloured fox dubbing or Fly-Rite
Wings: pale yellow-brown mallard
Hackle: pale ginger cock hackle

Irresistible

A deer-hair fly for fast-flowing water, this floats like a cork.

Tail: a thick bunch of deer or bucktail hairs
Body: clipped deer-hair
Wings: deer or bucktail hair, parted in a V-shape
Hackle: dark blue dun

Adams

This is another American dry fly, but has wings made of hackle tips.

Tail: grizzly and ginger cock hackle fibres
Body: grey fur dubbing or Fly-Rite
Wings: grizzly hackle tips
Hackle: one grizzly, and one medium to dark ginger, cock hackle mixed together

Humpy

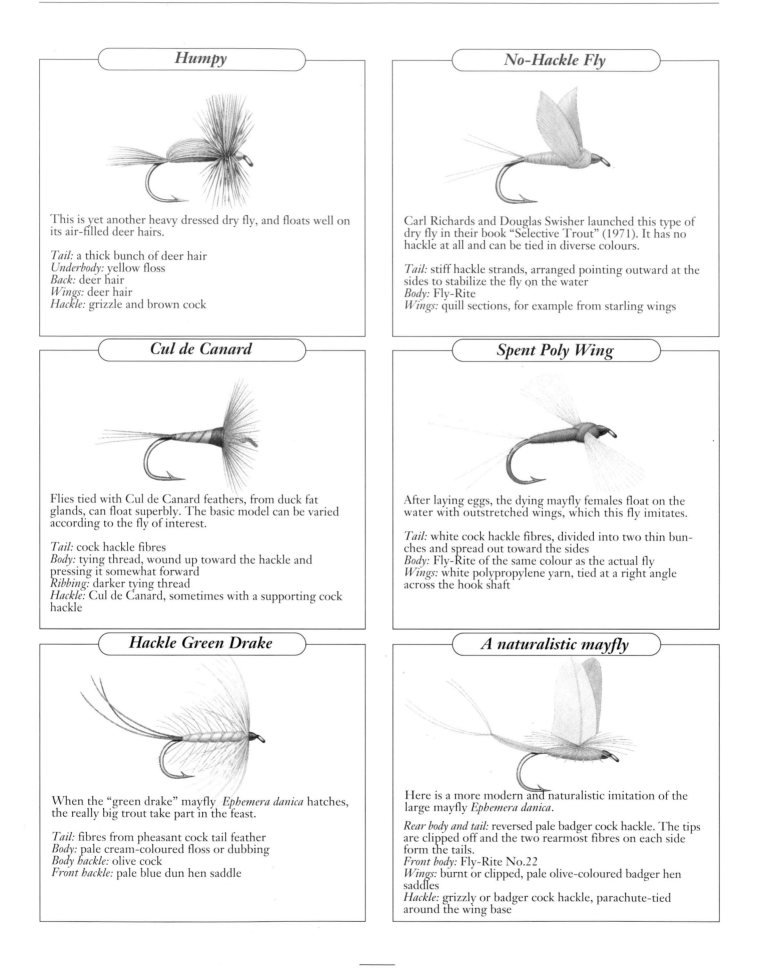

This is yet another heavy dressed dry fly, and floats well on its air-filled deer hairs.

Tail: a thick bunch of deer hair
Underbody: yellow floss
Back: deer hair
Wings: deer hair
Hackle: grizzle and brown cock

No-Hackle Fly

Carl Richards and Douglas Swisher launched this type of dry fly in their book "Selective Trout" (1971). It has no hackle at all and can be tied in diverse colours.

Tail: stiff hackle strands, arranged pointing outward at the sides to stabilize the fly on the water
Body: Fly-Rite
Wings: quill sections, for example from starling wings

Cul de Canard

Flies tied with Cul de Canard feathers, from duck fat glands, can float superbly. The basic model can be varied according to the fly of interest.

Tail: cock hackle fibres
Body: tying thread, wound up toward the hackle and pressing it somewhat forward
Ribbing: darker tying thread
Hackle: Cul de Canard, sometimes with a supporting cock hackle

Spent Poly Wing

After laying eggs, the dying mayfly females float on the water with outstretched wings, which this fly imitates.

Tail: white cock hackle fibres, divided into two thin bunches and spread out toward the sides
Body: Fly-Rite of the same colour as the actual fly
Wings: white polypropylene yarn, tied at a right angle across the hook shaft

Hackle Green Drake

When the "green drake" mayfly *Ephemera danica* hatches, the really big trout take part in the feast.

Tail: fibres from pheasant cock tail feather
Body: pale cream-coloured floss or dubbing
Body hackle: olive cock
Front hackle: pale blue dun hen saddle

A naturalistic mayfly

Here is a more modern and naturalistic imitation of the large mayfly *Ephemera danica*.

Rear body and tail: reversed pale badger cock hackle. The tips are clipped off and the two rearmost fibres on each side form the tails.
Front body: Fly-Rite No.22
Wings: burnt or clipped, pale olive-coloured badger hen saddles
Hackle: grizzly or badger cock hackle, parachute-tied around the fly wing base

Winged Caddis Flies

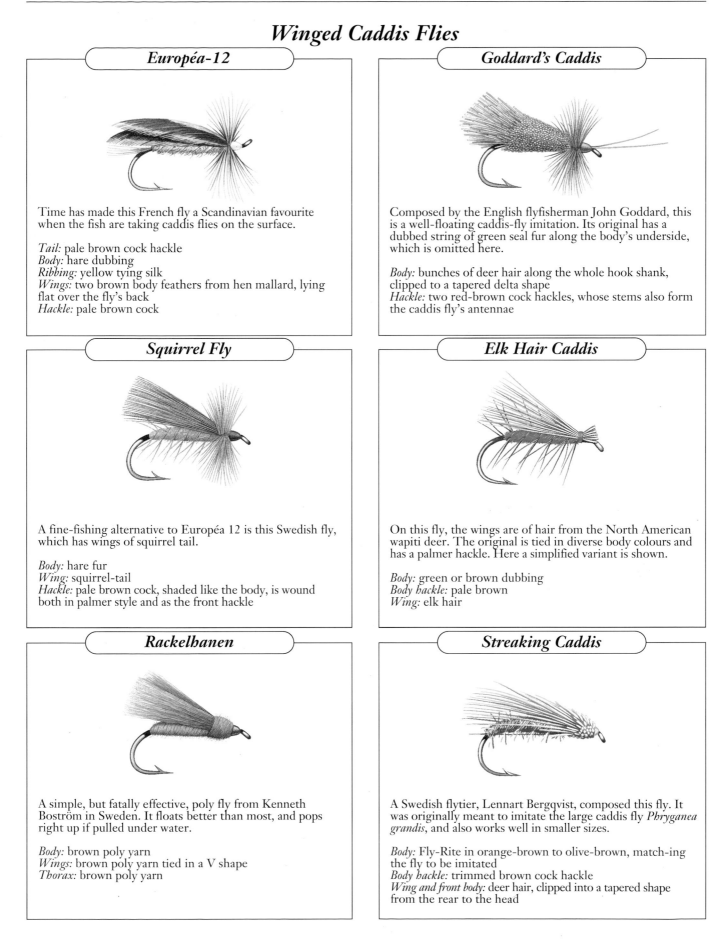

Európéa-12

Time has made this French fly a Scandinavian favourite when the fish are taking caddis flies on the surface.

Tail: pale brown cock hackle
Body: hare dubbing
Ribbing: yellow tying silk
Wings: two brown body feathers from hen mallard, lying flat over the fly's back
Hackle: pale brown cock

Goddard's Caddis

Composed by the English flyfisherman John Goddard, this is a well-floating caddis-fly imitation. Its original has a dubbed string of green seal fur along the body's underside, which is omitted here.

Body: bunches of deer hair along the whole hook shank, clipped to a tapered delta shape
Hackle: two red-brown cock hackles, whose stems also form the caddis fly's antennae

Squirrel Fly

A fine-fishing alternative to Európéa 12 is this Swedish fly, which has wings of squirrel tail.

Body: hare fur
Wing: squirrel-tail
Hackle: pale brown cock, shaded like the body, is wound both in palmer style and as the front hackle

Elk Hair Caddis

On this fly, the wings are of hair from the North American wapiti deer. The original is tied in diverse body colours and has a palmer hackle. Here a simplified variant is shown.

Body: green or brown dubbing
Body hackle: pale brown
Wing: elk hair

Rackelhanen

A simple, but fatally effective, poly fly from Kenneth Boström in Sweden. It floats better than most, and pops right up if pulled under water.

Body: brown poly yarn
Wings: brown poly yarn tied in a V shape
Thorax: brown poly yarn

Streaking Caddis

A Swedish flytier, Lennart Bergqvist, composed this fly. It was originally meant to imitate the large caddis fly *Phryganea grandis*, and also works well in smaller sizes.

Body: Fly-Rite in orange-brown to olive-brown, match-ing the fly to be imitated
Body hackle: trimmed brown cock hackle
Wing and front body: deer hair, clipped into a tapered shape from the rear to the head

Nymphs

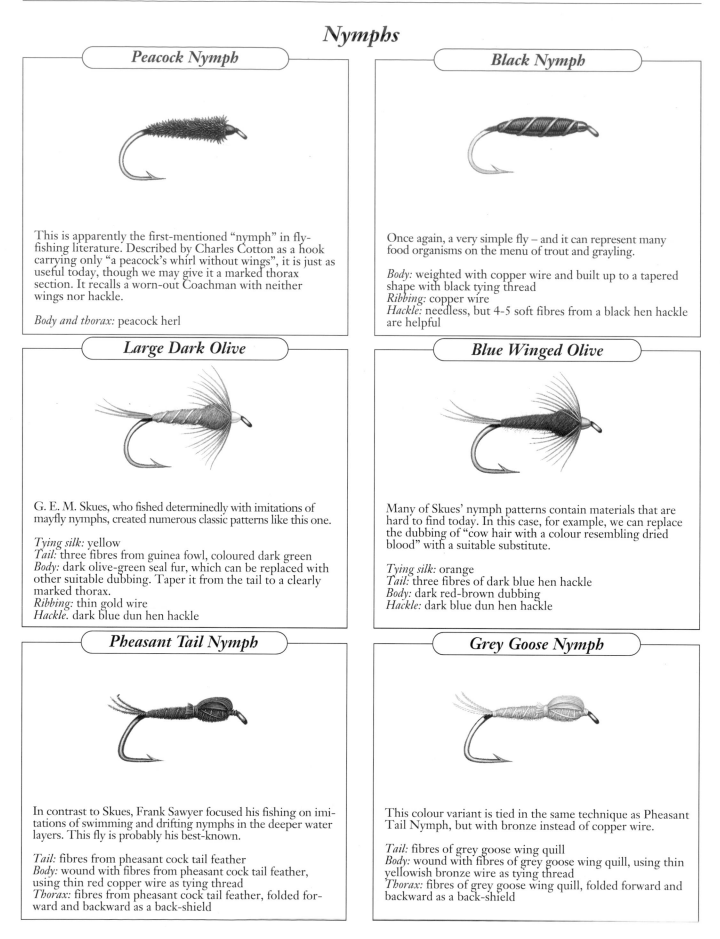

Peacock Nymph

This is apparently the first-mentioned "nymph" in fly-fishing literature. Described by Charles Cotton as a hook carrying only "a peacock's whirl without wings", it is just as useful today, though we may give it a marked thorax section. It recalls a worn-out Coachman with neither wings nor hackle.

Body and thorax: peacock herl

Black Nymph

Once again, a very simple fly – and it can represent many food organisms on the menu of trout and grayling.

Body: weighted with copper wire and built up to a tapered shape with black tying thread
Ribbing: copper wire
Hackle: needless, but 4-5 soft fibres from a black hen hackle are helpful

Large Dark Olive

G. E. M. Skues, who fished determinedly with imitations of mayfly nymphs, created numerous classic patterns like this one.

Tying silk: yellow
Tail: three fibres from guinea fowl, coloured dark green
Body: dark olive-green seal fur, which can be replaced with other suitable dubbing. Taper it from the tail to a clearly marked thorax.
Ribbing: thin gold wire
Hackle: dark blue dun hen hackle

Blue Winged Olive

Many of Skues' nymph patterns contain materials that are hard to find today. In this case, for example, we can replace the dubbing of "cow hair with a colour resembling dried blood" with a suitable substitute.

Tying silk: orange
Tail: three fibres of dark blue hen hackle
Body: dark red-brown dubbing
Hackle: dark blue dun hen hackle

Pheasant Tail Nymph

In contrast to Skues, Frank Sawyer focused his fishing on imitations of swimming and drifting nymphs in the deeper water layers. This fly is probably his best-known.

Tail: fibres from pheasant cock tail feather
Body: wound with fibres from pheasant cock tail feather, using thin red copper wire as tying thread
Thorax: fibres from pheasant cock tail feather, folded forward and backward as a back-shield

Grey Goose Nymph

This colour variant is tied in the same technique as Pheasant Tail Nymph, but with bronze instead of copper wire.

Tail: fibres of grey goose wing quill
Body: wound with fibres of grey goose wing quill, using thin yellowish bronze wire as tying thread
Thorax: fibres of grey goose wing quill, folded forward and backward as a back-shield

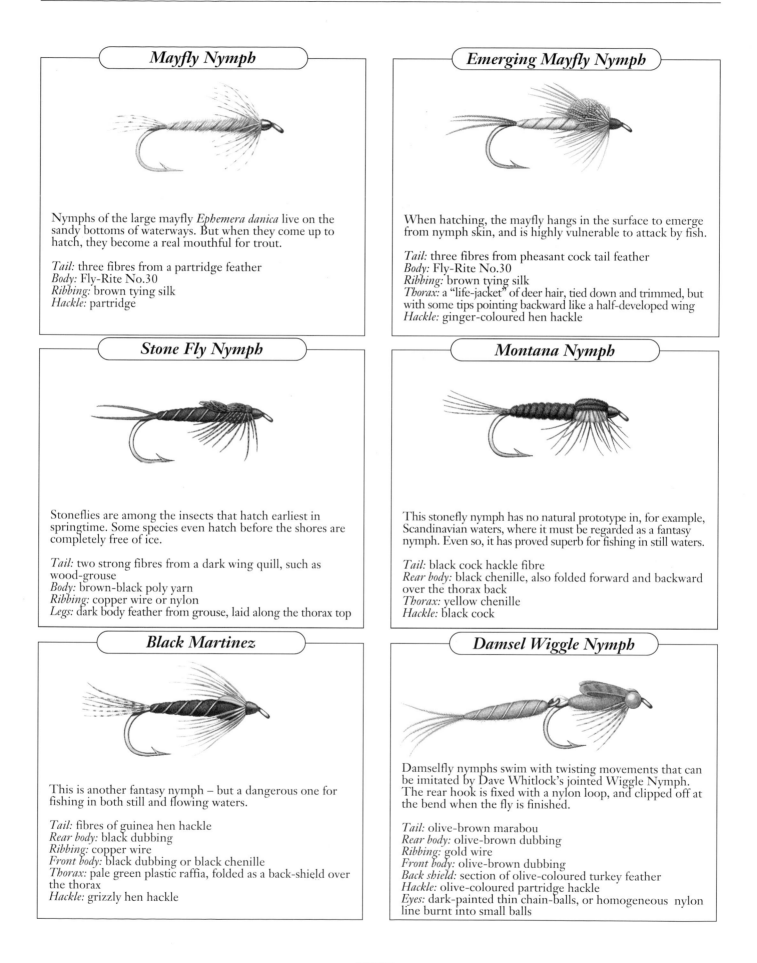

Mayfly Nymph

Nymphs of the large mayfly *Ephemera danica* live on the sandy bottoms of waterways. But when they come up to hatch, they become a real mouthful for trout.

Tail: three fibres from a partridge feather
Body: Fly-Rite No.30
Ribbing: brown tying silk
Hackle: partridge

Emerging Mayfly Nymph

When hatching, the mayfly hangs in the surface to emerge from nymph skin, and is highly vulnerable to attack by fish.

Tail: three fibres from pheasant cock tail feather
Body: Fly-Rite No.30
Ribbing: brown tying silk
Thorax: a "life-jacket" of deer hair, tied down and trimmed, but with some tips pointing backward like a half-developed wing
Hackle: ginger-coloured hen hackle

Stone Fly Nymph

Stoneflies are among the insects that hatch earliest in springtime. Some species even hatch before the shores are completely free of ice.

Tail: two strong fibres from a dark wing quill, such as wood-grouse
Body: brown-black poly yarn
Ribbing: copper wire or nylon
Legs: dark body feather from grouse, laid along the thorax top

Montana Nymph

This stonefly nymph has no natural prototype in, for example, Scandinavian waters, where it must be regarded as a fantasy nymph. Even so, it has proved superb for fishing in still waters.

Tail: black cock hackle fibre
Rear body: black chenille, also folded forward and backward over the thorax back
Thorax: yellow chenille
Hackle: black cock

Black Martinez

This is another fantasy nymph – but a dangerous one for fishing in both still and flowing waters.

Tail: fibres of guinea hen hackle
Rear body: black dubbing
Ribbing: copper wire
Front body: black dubbing or black chenille
Thorax: pale green plastic raffia, folded as a back-shield over the thorax
Hackle: grizzly hen hackle

Damsel Wiggle Nymph

Damselfly nymphs swim with twisting movements that can be imitated by Dave Whitlock's jointed Wiggle Nymph. The rear hook is fixed with a nylon loop, and clipped off at the bend when the fly is finished.

Tail: olive-brown marabou
Rear body: olive-brown dubbing
Ribbing: gold wire
Front body: olive-brown dubbing
Back shield: section of olive-coloured turkey feather
Hackle: olive-coloured partridge hackle
Eyes: dark-painted thin chain-balls, or homogeneous nylon line burnt into small balls

Flymphs and spiders

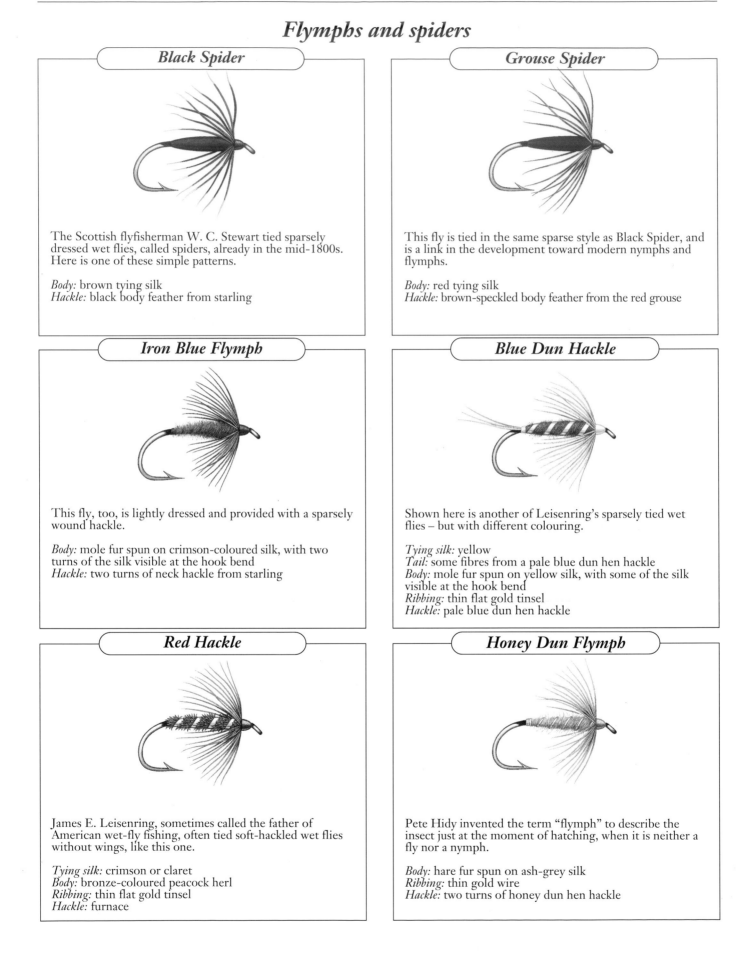

Black Spider

The Scottish flyfisherman W. C. Stewart tied sparsely dressed wet flies, called spiders, already in the mid-1800s. Here is one of these simple patterns.

Body: brown tying silk
Hackle: black body feather from starling

Grouse Spider

This fly is tied in the same sparse style as Black Spider, and is a link in the development toward modern nymphs and flymphs.

Body: red tying silk
Hackle: brown-speckled body feather from the red grouse

Iron Blue Flymph

This fly, too, is lightly dressed and provided with a sparsely wound hackle.

Body: mole fur spun on crimson-coloured silk, with two turns of the silk visible at the hook bend
Hackle: two turns of neck hackle from starling

Blue Dun Hackle

Shown here is another of Leisenring's sparsely tied wet flies – but with different colouring.

Tying silk: yellow
Tail: some fibres from a pale blue dun hen hackle
Body: mole fur spun on yellow silk, with some of the silk visible at the hook bend
Ribbing: thin flat gold tinsel
Hackle: pale blue dun hen hackle

Red Hackle

James E. Leisenring, sometimes called the father of American wet-fly fishing, often tied soft-hackled wet flies without wings, like this one.

Tying silk: crimson or claret
Body: bronze-coloured peacock herl
Ribbing: thin flat gold tinsel
Hackle: furnace

Honey Dun Flymph

Pete Hidy invented the term "flymph" to describe the insect just at the moment of hatching, when it is neither a fly nor a nymph.

Body: hare fur spun on ash-grey silk
Ribbing: thin gold wire
Hackle: two turns of honey dun hen hackle

Midge pupae and caddis-fly larvae

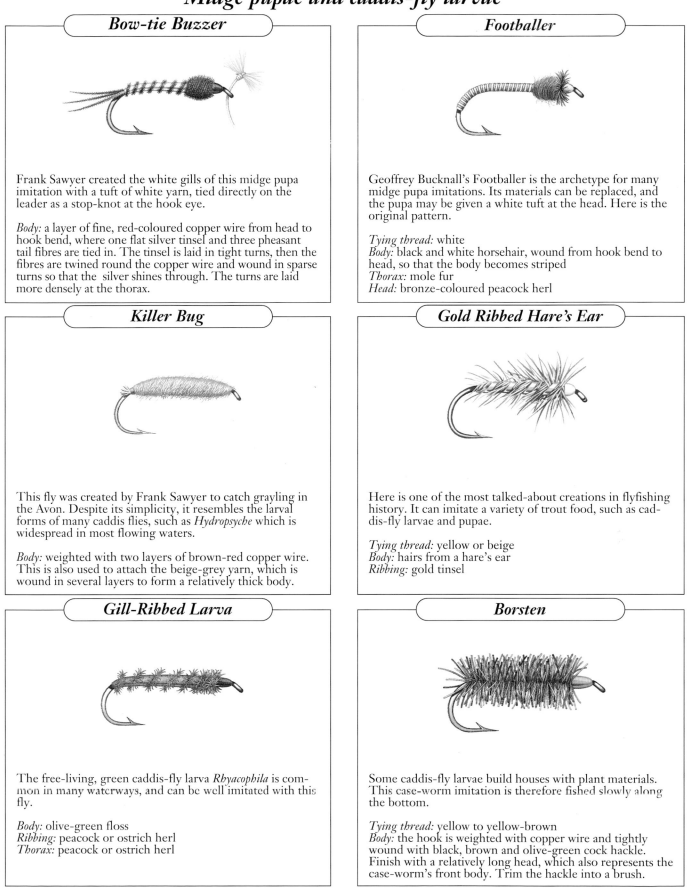

Bow-tie Buzzer

Frank Sawyer created the white gills of this midge pupa imitation with a tuft of white yarn, tied directly on the leader as a stop-knot at the hook eye.

Body: a layer of fine, red-coloured copper wire from head to hook bend, where one flat silver tinsel and three pheasant tail fibres are tied in. The tinsel is laid in tight turns, then the fibres are twined round the copper wire and wound in sparse turns so that the silver shines through. The turns are laid more densely at the thorax.

Footballer

Geoffrey Bucknall's Footballer is the archetype for many midge pupa imitations. Its materials can be replaced, and the pupa may be given a white tuft at the head. Here is the original pattern.

Tying thread: white
Body: black and white horsehair, wound from hook bend to head, so that the body becomes striped
Thorax: mole fur
Head: bronze-coloured peacock herl

Killer Bug

This fly was created by Frank Sawyer to catch grayling in the Avon. Despite its simplicity, it resembles the larval forms of many caddis flies, such as *Hydropsyche* which is widespread in most flowing waters.

Body: weighted with two layers of brown-red copper wire. This is also used to attach the beige-grey yarn, which is wound in several layers to form a relatively thick body.

Gold Ribbed Hare's Ear

Here is one of the most talked-about creations in flyfishing history. It can imitate a variety of trout food, such as caddis-fly larvae and pupae.

Tying thread: yellow or beige
Body: hairs from a hare's ear
Ribbing: gold tinsel

Gill-Ribbed Larva

The free-living, green caddis-fly larva *Rhyacophila* is common in many waterways, and can be well imitated with this fly.

Body: olive-green floss
Ribbing: peacock or ostrich herl
Thorax: peacock or ostrich herl

Borsten

Some caddis-fly larvae build houses with plant materials. This case-worm imitation is therefore fished slowly along the bottom.

Tying thread: yellow to yellow-brown
Body: the hook is weighted with copper wire and tightly wound with black, brown and olive-green cock hackle. Finish with a relatively long head, which also represents the case-worm's front body. Trim the hackle into a brush.

Caddis-fly pupae

Standardpupa

This is a basic model for a caddis-fly pupa. It can be fished weighted or unweighted, and varied in colour according to the species that are hatching.

Rear body: relatively thick, dubbed down in the hook bend
Ribbing: yellow tying thread
Thorax: darker dubbing, such as hare fur
Wing rudiments: a section of quill feather on each side
Hackle: soft hen or partridge hackle, coloured like the thorax

Deep Sparkle Pupa

The American flyfisherman Gary LaFontaine has studied the underwater forms of caddis flies, and composed several interesting patterns like this, in which he emphasizes the pupa's brightly shimmering abdomen.

Underbody: weighted and dubbed in the colour of the actual pupa's body
Outer body: bright sparkle yarn, tied in at the hook bend and folded forward like a bag round the body
Hackle: sparse hen hackle to imitate legs and antennae
Thorax: marabou fibres or dark dubbing

Emergent Sparkle Pupa

Gary LaFontaine also has this unweighted, hatching variant of the same pupa model.

Underbody: dubbed in the colour of the actual pupa
Outer body: bright sparkle yarn, tied like a bag but with a few loose fibres pointing backward
Wing: deer hair
Thorax: marabou fibres or dark dubbing

Simo Lummes Pupa

This Finnish caddis-fly pupa is composed along the same lines as Gary LaFontaine's, and is tied with shiny antron yarn. The dubbing is picked out from under the silver ribbing and brushed back with a toothbrush, before the thorax's hare dubbing is varnished and stroked backward.

Rear body: dubbed in the same colour as the prototype
Ribbing: relatively thick round silver tinsel
Front body: hare dubbing

Green Caddis-Fly Flymph

A lively flymph, specially created to catch grayling when caddis flies are hatching. Its body holds many small air bubbles.

Rear body: olive-green rabbit fur on yellow silk
Ribbing: thin gold wire
Front body: dark brown hare fur
Hackle: partridge

Superpupa

One of the Swedish flytier Lennart Bergqvist's creations: a floating caddis-fly pupa which has plenty of fish on its conscience.

Rear body: Fly-Rite in the prototype's colour
Front body: darker Fly-Rite in the prototype's colour
Hackle: cock hackle in the same basic shade as the pupa, tied in palmer style and clipped on the top and bottom, so that it protrudes only at the sides

Terrestrials

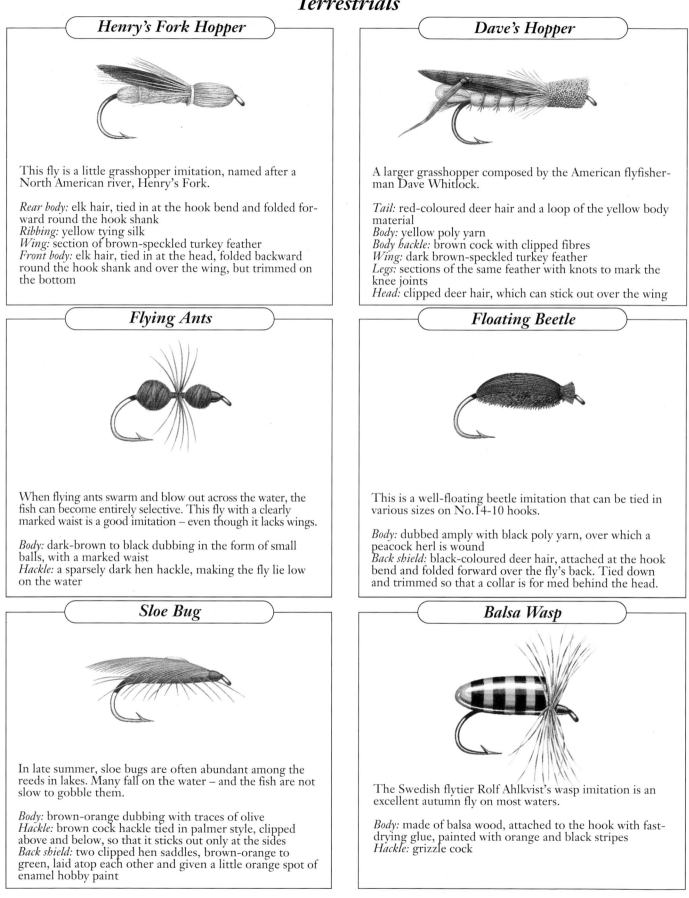

Henry's Fork Hopper

This fly is a little grasshopper imitation, named after a North American river, Henry's Fork.

Rear body: elk hair, tied in at the hook bend and folded forward round the hook shank
Ribbing: yellow tying silk
Wing: section of brown-speckled turkey feather
Front body: elk hair, tied in at the head, folded backward round the hook shank and over the wing, but trimmed on the bottom

Dave's Hopper

A larger grasshopper composed by the American flyfisherman Dave Whitlock.

Tail: red-coloured deer hair and a loop of the yellow body material
Body: yellow poly yarn
Body hackle: brown cock with clipped fibres
Wing: dark brown-speckled turkey feather
Legs: sections of the same feather with knots to mark the knee joints
Head: clipped deer hair, which can stick out over the wing

Flying Ants

When flying ants swarm and blow out across the water, the fish can become entirely selective. This fly with a clearly marked waist is a good imitation – even though it lacks wings.

Body: dark-brown to black dubbing in the form of small balls, with a marked waist
Hackle: a sparsely dark hen hackle, making the fly lie low on the water

Floating Beetle

This is a well-floating beetle imitation that can be tied in various sizes on No.14-10 hooks.

Body: dubbed amply with black poly yarn, over which a peacock herl is wound
Back shield: black-coloured deer hair, attached at the hook bend and folded forward over the fly's back. Tied down and trimmed so that a collar is for med behind the head.

Sloe Bug

In late summer, sloe bugs are often abundant among the reeds in lakes. Many fall on the water – and the fish are not slow to gobble them.

Body: brown-orange dubbing with traces of olive
Hackle: brown cock hackle tied in palmer style, clipped above and below, so that it sticks out only at the sides
Back shield: two clipped hen saddles, brown-orange to green, laid atop each other and given a little orange spot of enamel hobby paint

Balsa Wasp

The Swedish flytier Rolf Ahlkvist's wasp imitation is an excellent autumn fly on most waters.

Body: made of balsa wood, attached to the hook with fast-drying glue, painted with orange and black stripes
Hackle: grizzle cock

Streamers

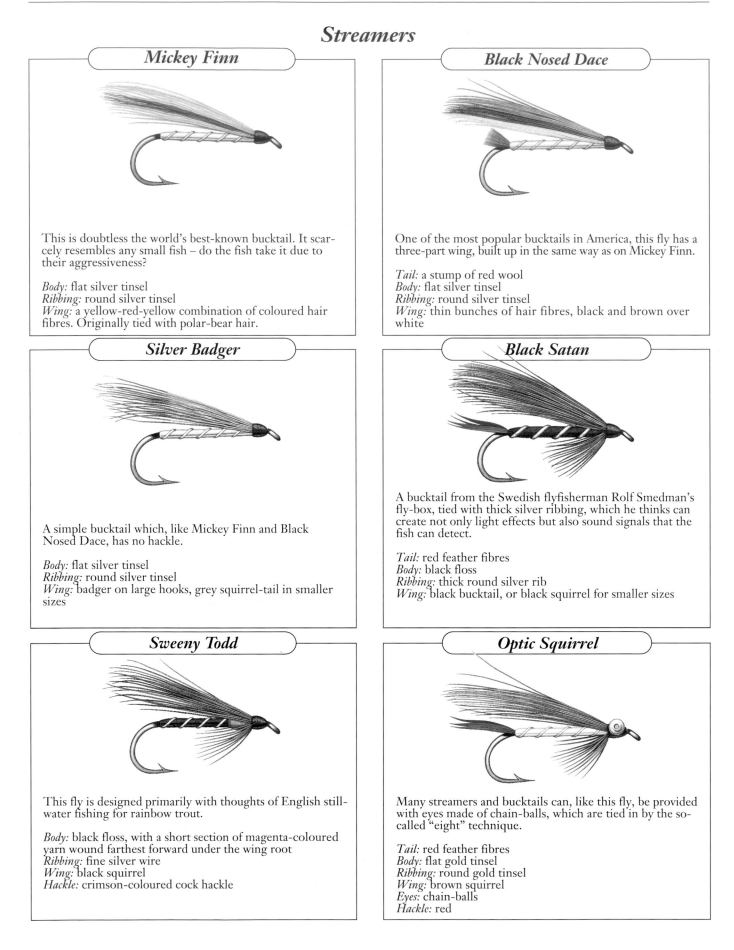

Mickey Finn

This is doubtless the world's best-known bucktail. It scarcely resembles any small fish – do the fish take it due to their aggressiveness?

Body: flat silver tinsel
Ribbing: round silver tinsel
Wing: a yellow-red-yellow combination of coloured hair fibres. Originally tied with polar-bear hair.

Black Nosed Dace

One of the most popular bucktails in America, this fly has a three-part wing, built up in the same way as on Mickey Finn.

Tail: a stump of red wool
Body: flat silver tinsel
Ribbing: round silver tinsel
Wing: thin bunches of hair fibres, black and brown over white

Silver Badger

A simple bucktail which, like Mickey Finn and Black Nosed Dace, has no hackle.

Body: flat silver tinsel
Ribbing: round silver tinsel
Wing: badger on large hooks, grey squirrel-tail in smaller sizes

Black Satan

A bucktail from the Swedish flyfisherman Rolf Smedman's fly-box, tied with thick silver ribbing, which he thinks can create not only light effects but also sound signals that the fish can detect.

Tail: red feather fibres
Body: black floss
Ribbing: thick round silver rib
Wing: black bucktail, or black squirrel for smaller sizes

Sweeny Todd

This fly is designed primarily with thoughts of English still-water fishing for rainbow trout.

Body: black floss, with a short section of magenta-coloured yarn wound farthest forward under the wing root
Ribbing: fine silver wire
Wing: black squirrel
Hackle: crimson-coloured cock hackle

Optic Squirrel

Many streamers and bucktails can, like this fly, be provided with eyes made of chain-balls, which are tied in by the so-called "eight" technique.

Tail: red feather fibres
Body: flat gold tinsel
Ribbing: round gold tinsel
Wing: brown squirrel
Eyes: chain-balls
Hackle: red

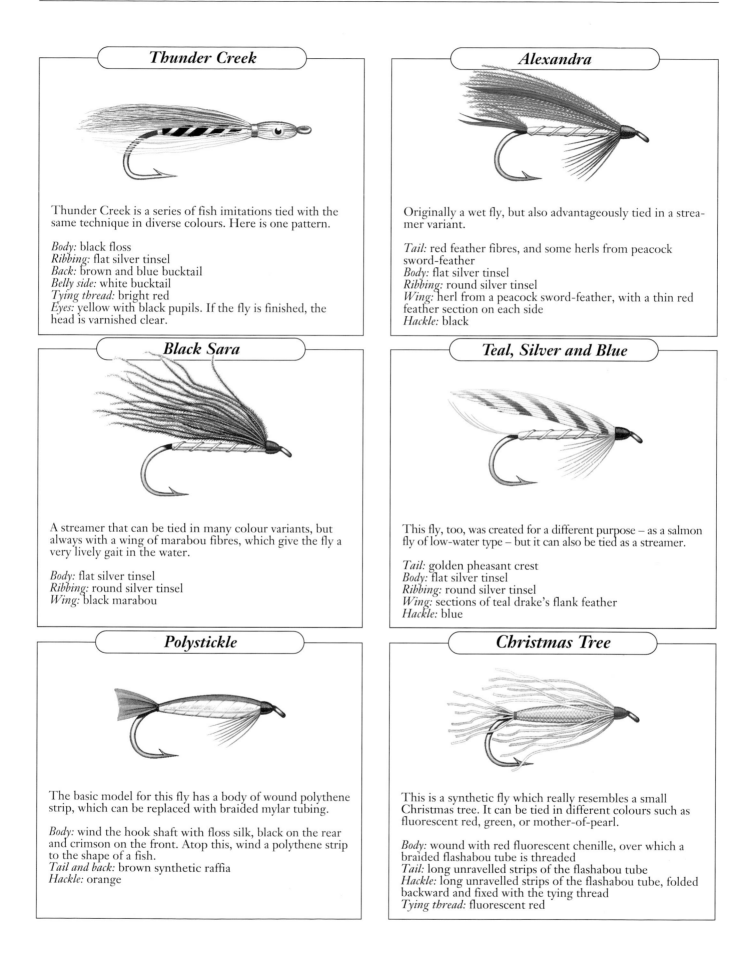

Thunder Creek

Thunder Creek is a series of fish imitations tied with the same technique in diverse colours. Here is one pattern.

Body: black floss
Ribbing: flat silver tinsel
Back: brown and blue bucktail
Belly side: white bucktail
Tying thread: bright red
Eyes: yellow with black pupils. If the fly is finished, the head is varnished clear.

Alexandra

Originally a wet fly, but also advantageously tied in a streamer variant.

Tail: red feather fibres, and some herls from peacock sword-feather
Body: flat silver tinsel
Ribbing: round silver tinsel
Wing: herl from a peacock sword-feather, with a thin red feather section on each side
Hackle: black

Black Sara

A streamer that can be tied in many colour variants, but always with a wing of marabou fibres, which give the fly a very lively gait in the water.

Body: flat silver tinsel
Ribbing: round silver tinsel
Wing: black marabou

Teal, Silver and Blue

This fly, too, was created for a different purpose – as a salmon fly of low-water type – but it can also be tied as a streamer.

Tail: golden pheasant crest
Body: flat silver tinsel
Ribbing: round silver tinsel
Wing: sections of teal drake's flank feather
Hackle: blue

Polystickle

The basic model for this fly has a body of wound polythene strip, which can be replaced with braided mylar tubing.

Body: wind the hook shaft with floss silk, black on the rear and crimson on the front. Atop this, wind a polythene strip to the shape of a fish.
Tail and back: brown synthetic raffia
Hackle: orange

Christmas Tree

This is a synthetic fly which really resembles a small Christmas tree. It can be tied in different colours such as fluorescent red, green, or mother-of-pearl.

Body: wound with red fluorescent chenille, over which a braided flashabou tube is threaded
Tail: long unravelled strips of the flashabou tube
Hackle: long unravelled strips of the flashabou tube, folded backward and fixed with the tying thread
Tying thread: fluorescent red

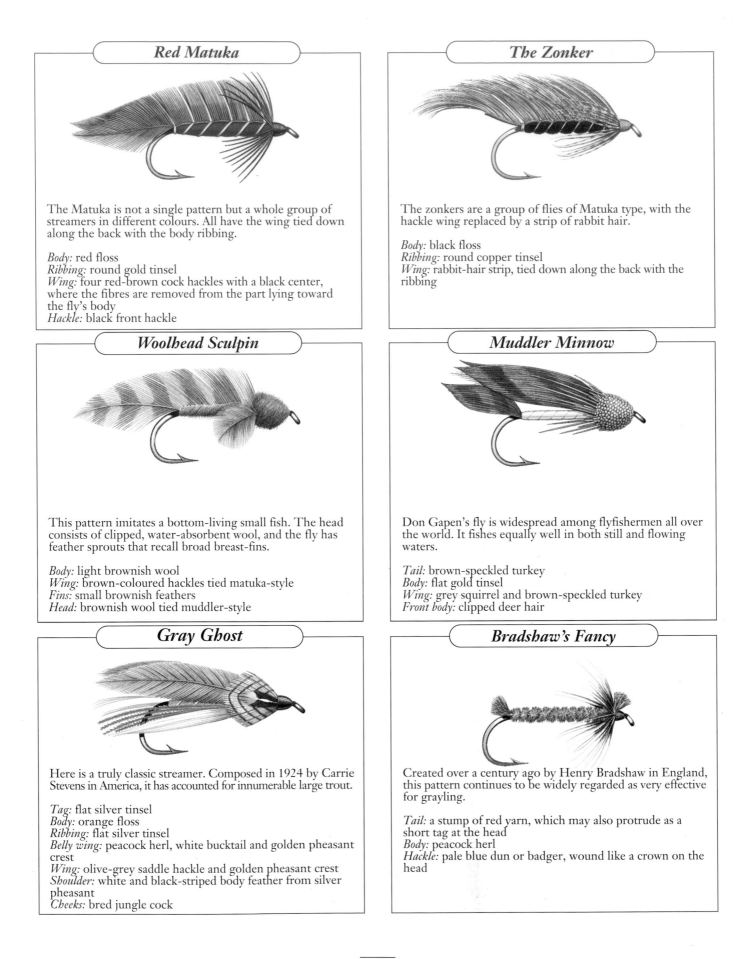

Red Matuka

The Matuka is not a single pattern but a whole group of streamers in different colours. All have the wing tied down along the back with the body ribbing.

Body: red floss
Ribbing: round gold tinsel
Wing: four red-brown cock hackles with a black center, where the fibres are removed from the part lying toward the fly's body
Hackle: black front hackle

The Zonker

The zonkers are a group of flies of Matuka type, with the hackle wing replaced by a strip of rabbit hair.

Body: black floss
Ribbing: round copper tinsel
Wing: rabbit-hair strip, tied down along the back with the ribbing

Woolhead Sculpin

This pattern imitates a bottom-living small fish. The head consists of clipped, water-absorbent wool, and the fly has feather sprouts that recall broad breast-fins.

Body: light brownish wool
Wing: brown-coloured hackles tied matuka-style
Fins: small brownish feathers
Head: brownish wool tied muddler-style

Muddler Minnow

Don Gapen's fly is widespread among flyfishermen all over the world. It fishes equally well in both still and flowing waters.

Tail: brown-speckled turkey
Body: flat gold tinsel
Wing: grey squirrel and brown-speckled turkey
Front body: clipped deer hair

Gray Ghost

Here is a truly classic streamer. Composed in 1924 by Carrie Stevens in America, it has accounted for innumerable large trout.

Tag: flat silver tinsel
Body: orange floss
Ribbing: flat silver tinsel
Belly wing: peacock herl, white bucktail and golden pheasant crest
Wing: olive-grey saddle hackle and golden pheasant crest
Shoulder: white and black-striped body feather from silver pheasant
Cheeks: bred jungle cock

Bradshaw's Fancy

Created over a century ago by Henry Bradshaw in England, this pattern continues to be widely regarded as very effective for grayling.

Tail: a stump of red yarn, which may also protrude as a short tag at the head
Body: peacock herl
Hackle: pale blue dun or badger, wound like a crown on the head

Other patterns

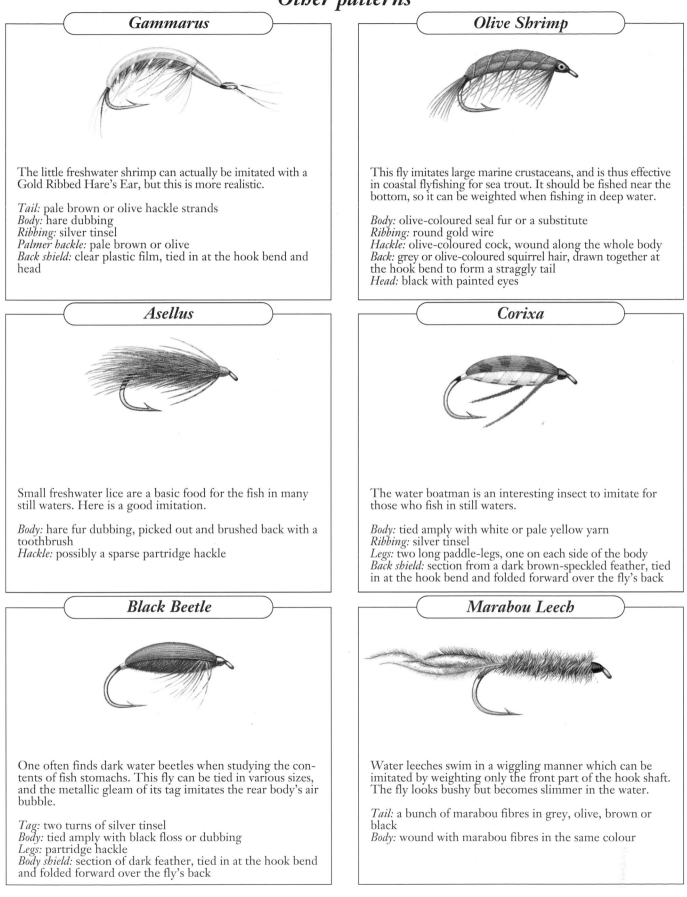

Gammarus

The little freshwater shrimp can actually be imitated with a Gold Ribbed Hare's Ear, but this is more realistic.

Tail: pale brown or olive hackle strands
Body: hare dubbing
Ribbing: silver tinsel
Palmer hackle: pale brown or olive
Back shield: clear plastic film, tied in at the hook bend and head

Olive Shrimp

This fly imitates large marine crustaceans, and is thus effective in coastal flyfishing for sea trout. It should be fished near the bottom, so it can be weighted when fishing in deep water.

Body: olive-coloured seal fur or a substitute
Ribbing: round gold wire
Hackle: olive-coloured cock, wound along the whole body
Back: grey or olive-coloured squirrel hair, drawn together at the hook bend to form a straggly tail
Head: black with painted eyes

Asellus

Small freshwater lice are a basic food for the fish in many still waters. Here is a good imitation.

Body: hare fur dubbing, picked out and brushed back with a toothbrush
Hackle: possibly a sparse partridge hackle

Corixa

The water boatman is an interesting insect to imitate for those who fish in still waters.

Body: tied amply with white or pale yellow yarn
Ribbing: silver tinsel
Legs: two long paddle-legs, one on each side of the body
Back shield: section from a dark brown-speckled feather, tied in at the hook bend and folded forward over the fly's back

Black Beetle

One often finds dark water beetles when studying the contents of fish stomachs. This fly can be tied in various sizes, and the metallic gleam of its tag imitates the rear body's air bubble.

Tag: two turns of silver tinsel
Body: tied amply with black floss or dubbing
Legs: partridge hackle
Body shield: section of dark feather, tied in at the hook bend and folded forward over the fly's back

Marabou Leech

Water leeches swim in a wiggling manner which can be imitated by weighting only the front part of the hook shaft. The fly looks bushy but becomes slimmer in the water.

Tail: a bunch of marabou fibres in grey, olive, brown or black
Body: wound with marabou fibres in the same colour

Wet-fly
Fishing

It is generally believed that the first flyfishing was done with wet flies. This may be true, although we cannot be sure, as the origins of the sport are documented only by brief fragments in early historical writings. The oldest flies were very simple, and today one can only speculate about whether they were fished as wet or dry flies. Probably both – they sometimes floated, and sometimes sank! In any case, farther along towards our own age, there are actual descriptions suggesting that dry-fly fishing came first, contrary to the usual opinion.

Dame Juliana Berners' book "A Treatyse of Fysshynge wyth an Angle" (1496) gives a short treatment of fishing with artificial flies. And with Izaak Walton's "The Compleat Angler" (1653), a more detailed record of the period's fishing with artificial flies became available. Here the author showed quite clearly how flyfishing was done. This overthrows the theory that wet-fly fishing had to be the pioneering method, and that dry-fly fishing developed in the following centuries.

The three ways of fishing

Moreover, Walton's presentation of different fly patterns, and of the equipment used, virtually repeated Dame Juliana's text. So his fishing techniques could well have been at least 200 years old. Walton stated, too, that sportsmanlike fishing with a rod possessed three ways of fishing: fishing "upon" or "on top of" the water, fishing at the bottom, and fishing in the middle. The latter types were entirely reserved for angling with worms or small baitfish.

Thus, already in those days, flyfishing was exclusively a method for fishing on the water surface – in effect, a kind of dry-fly fishing. Nowhere was it maintained that one could also fish with wet flies. Walton emphasized this distinction by saying: "No portion of the line or leader should touch the water when flyfishing."

Instead, one was expected to keep the rod lifted and guide the fly so that it danced on the surface.

In later editions of Walton's book, some chapters were added with more specific instructions about fishing with artificial flies. Their author, Charles Cotton, supplied further details and told not only how such flies were tied, but how they were cast. Even he, though, defined flyfishing as a sport on the water surface.

It is interesting to compare a still older work, "El Manuscrito de Astorga" (1624), dealing with flies in Spain. According to the preface, the described flies had previously been assumed to be wet flies, but studies had revealed that at least some of them should be regarded as what we would term "dry flies".

Sparsely dressed flies

Fishermen in Walton's day used a long rod with a top-knotted line, and therefore tried actively to make their artificial flies attract the fish up to the water surface. However, we can easily imagine that the fly soon absorbed water. Occasionally it would sink and could be fished as a wet fly, so that the line between dry-fly and wet-fly fishing probably became rather fuzzy with the years. In a word, people fished with flies, avoiding the division into dry-fly and wet-fly methods which has been laid down by subsequent flyfishermen.

During the same seventeenth century, flies were tied in order to imitate specific, named insects, which hatched at various times of the season. Gradually different types of flies were invented, taking account of both the insects' appearance and the proper way to fish them.

The wet flies sank more easily if they were tied on hooks with a thick shank, were sparsely dressed, and had a profile that gave what the English call "a good

Already during the 16th and 17th centuries – in Izaak Walton's time – there was much discussion of fishing flies, and they were frequently more sophisticated than we think. Walton recognized the "three departments" of fish: at the water surface, in the middle layer, and at the bottom. Fishing on the surface had to be done primarily with flies. But when dry flies sank, as they inevitably did when water-absorbent, they could also be fished as wet flies.

Before long, flies began to be tied that were specially intended for fishing under the surface, and development of wet-fly fishing began. Wet flies were then tied sparsely on heavy books, and it was essential that they should give a "good entry", which called for stream-lined bodies with back-swept wings.

entry". This meant having a streamlined shape, and a backward-turned wing for easy penetration of the water surface. By contrast, the dry flies were tied on light hooks made of thin gauge wire, and had upright wings. Eventually they were also given a wound hackle, to increase their area for support against the surface. Like earlier dry flies, the wet flies were often tied to imitate some specific insect. But a variety of fantasy flies also proved themselves able to catch fish.

Sinking flies

There were now two ways of fishing with a fly, and the opposition between wet-fly and dry-fly fishing arose. It had not existed at the time of Walton, when primitive "dry-fly angling" ruled the ripples – although we can see from contemporary tying instructions that the flies were perhaps more similar in character to modern wet flies. Nor were Walton's winged dry flies provided with hackles. These occurred only on so-called Palmer flies, which had no wings and just a sparse, spiral-wound hackle along the whole body, as on the Palmer flies that we tie today.

Against this background, it is easy to understand how such winged but unhackled flies often sank and, therefore, led to fishing with wet flies. Besides, for historical reasons, the tradition of Walton was presumably lost in the course of centuries, and our two forms of flyfishing came to live side by side.

Developing the equipment

Fishing with wet flies, however, gave rise to particular requirements for its practitioners. With a wet fly, one no longer fished only in a flat plane on the water surface, but also in a third dimension, down deep, which demanded a new fishing technique. It was not enough to "dip" the fly and keep the line clear of the water. Instead the line's end had to sink, while the rest of the line floated largely on the surface. The water flow influenced the line in both horizontal and vertical directions. The fisherman, aided by the rod, was forced to guide the line – and thus the fly – so that it fished at the correct level and in the correct manner, inspiring confidence in the fish and persuading them to strike.

Necessary improvements

Consequently, wet-fly fishing asked for a good deal more effort than did Walton's relatively simple surface-angling with flies that hopped and danced. His method involved a short fishing distance, and little trouble in keeping an eye on the flies. But the wet-fly fisherman lost sight of the fly in the water, and had to rely on his skill in guiding it with his rod to the holding place of the fish. Turbulent currents underwater caused problems, and surface currents of varying speed tended to pull the line in an arc downstream. Then the fly was pulled up until it dragged in the surface.

The inevitable result was that wet-fly fishing called for better equipment, which allowed the fly to be cast with a greater line length than in surface-angling. The rod had to be soft enough for longer performance, more sweeping casts, and an ability to mend the line. In time, the line could also be fed out from a primitive reel. Walton himself described such reels, but said that they were very uncommon. The evolution of equipment, and next of casting techniques, was therefore essential for wet-fly fishing of the kind familiar to us.

The nature of wet flies

On the dry flies that sank underwater and began to fish like wet flies, the wings were pushed backward by the water pressure. So fishermen eventually started to tie flies with special profiles, which depended on how the fishing was to be done. Dry flies kept their upright wings, while the wet flies were tied with wings lying down over the hook shank. Moreover, the flies acquired hackles tied with material from diverse birds – a borrowing from the early Palmer flies.

Yet the developments were not identical in all parts of Europe. Even today, we can see distinctive tying styles on wet flies from different countries. Spain, for example, has unhackled wet flies that consist only of a body with a fan-shaped wing made of stiff rooster-hackle fibres lying on the back. In England, wet flies are tied with quill wings, and have a chin hackle of soft hen-hackle fibres. The Danes often prefer a stiffer front hackle from a rooster, tied in front of the wing.

In both England and America, there are also wet flies with so-called "bunch wings", made of segments from duck flank feathers, as in the well-known Teal

Flies have gradually been improved ever since the 16th century – a development that is still going on, and will continue to do so as long as there are flyfisherman on Earth. Shown below are some types of wet flies with proven records of success.

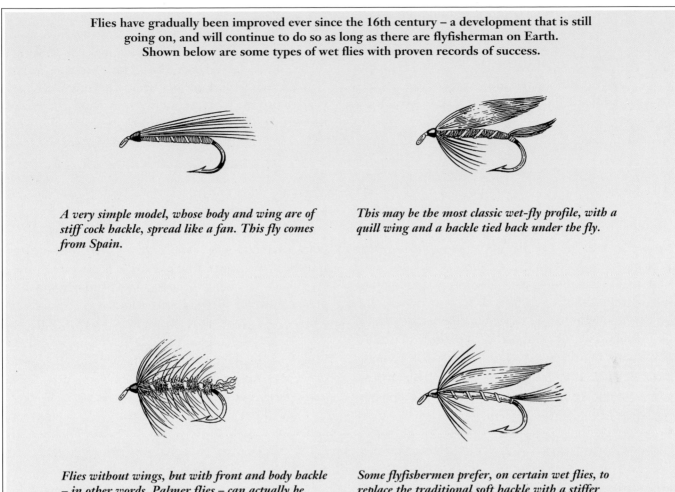

A very simple model, whose body and wing are of stiff cock hackle, spread like a fan. This fly comes from Spain.

This may be the most classic wet-fly profile, with a quill wing and a hackle tied back under the fly.

Flies without wings, but with front and body hackle – in other words, Palmer flies – can actually be fished as both dry and wet flies, and perhaps once were.

Some flyfishermen prefer, on certain wet flies, to replace the traditional soft hackle with a stiffer hackle wound as a collar.

The well-known Teal series, with flank feather from a teal duck, is a good example of bunch-winged wet flies. These give a more lively impression, not least in still waters.

This wingless, crown-hackled fly is a simple but effective type of wet fly. The hackle's stiffness can be adapted to the given current conditions.

series. In addition, we have the very old Palmer flies, which still look as they did in Walton's day. Their hackle is wound along the entire body and they lack wings. Other wet flies simply have the hackle wound immediately behind the head – such as the famous Red Tag and Black Zulu.

Spectacular features

Wet-fly fishing is best defined generally as fishing underwater, from just under the surface down to the bottom. The flies may be fished either as imitations of various insects or as pure fantasy flies.

Some insects lay their eggs by crawling into the water along a stone or plant. Others fall onto the water from surrounding vegetation, or after mating. Dead, drowned bugs will thus drift with the current, past the holding places of fish. Winged wet flies can be said to have originally imitated such drowned insects.

Walton was already a precise reporter of what the different kinds of flies should imitate. One had to go further than copying a fly which lived on the water at a particular time of the season. The artificial fly, he wrote, should resemble the insect that is on the water during the very day one is fishing. However, flies were later developed which had no living prototype and turned out to fish well anyhow. These are what we call "fantasy flies". They attract fish by having some spectacular feature of dress, or by provoking the fish to become aggressive.

The importance of presentation

A wet fly does not fish solely with its appearance. It may appeal to the fish because it looks "insect-like", but the flyfisherman's way of using it is equally important. If it moves in a manner that is natural for drifting insects, the fish will think that the fly is a real one – even when its colour, shape and size differ from those of insects which the fish is accustomed to seeing in the

Wet flies are usually fished in flowing waters, and should thus imitate food that drifts downstream. Trout take passing food – or the drifting fly – from their holding places in the current.

(*Above*) *Traditional wet-fly fishing is directed downstream. Here the fly is presented on a stretch with a rolling bottom, full of possible holding places.*

When fishing in flowing water – as is typical with wet flies – the cast should be fished out completely. You cast obliquely downstream and let the fly drift until it hangs straight below you. By mending the line, you can correct for eddies and other current effects.

water. This is why the presentation of the fly has a fundamental impact and – in most cases – a greater one than the fly's appearance.

With few exceptions, wet flies are fished only in running waters, where trout take up holding positions and leave them occasionally to catch morsels of food that float by. A fish is reluctant to abandon its place in the current. Hence the flyfisherman has to cast, guide and present his fly so that it reaches the right level in the water, and follows a realistic trajectory past the fish's holding place. This requires not only an understanding of how fish choose holding places, and how they select food at the given time of year, but also an adequate range of equipment and plenty of practice with it.

Using your equipment

Trout fishing with wet flies is done with a one-handed rod. Normally the water is a rather small stream, and in a broad river you can wade into position. Your casts will therefore be short, and a relatively short rod of around 8 feet should suffice. But in wet-fly fishing, you must also steer the line on the water after the cast,

so that the leader will guide the fly to fish properly. Since this is easier to do with a longer rod, the usual choice is a rod of 9 feet or more.

Long rods with soft action

Modern rod materials have made it possible to manufacture long, but still light, fly rods – with good action in the line classes that are suitable for wet-fly fishing. Previously, long rods were heavy and cumbersome, wearing out the user's arms and back in the course of a fishing day. Long rods had to be heavy, as they were thick at the butt, and they did best with fairly heavy lines. If the rod was tapered more sharply, to decrease the weight and to take a lighter line, the rod lost its springiness and became too limp. By contrast, a long wooden rod could have good action only at the cost of being too heavy.

One-handed rods were consequently developed in ever shorter lengths, down to 7,5-8 feet, before graphite materials turned the trend upward again. These gave us, once again, somewhat longer rods that could guide the line better after the cast, yet were easy to handle and excellent for casting a light line of class 5-6. The

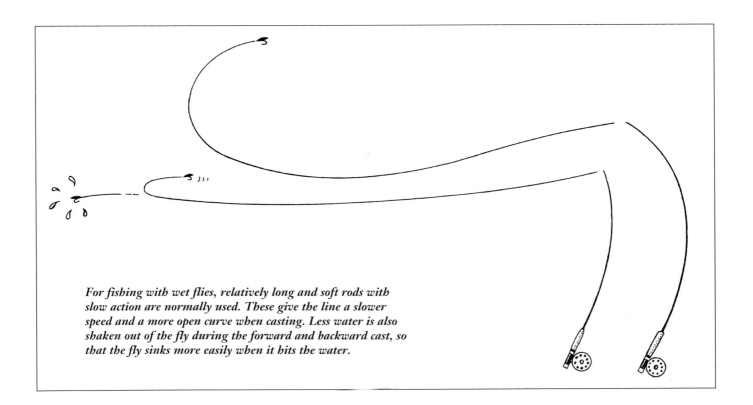

For fishing with wet flies, relatively long and soft rods with slow action are normally used. These give the line a slower speed and a more open curve when casting. Less water is also shaken out of the fly during the forward and backward cast, so that the fly sinks more easily when it hits the water.

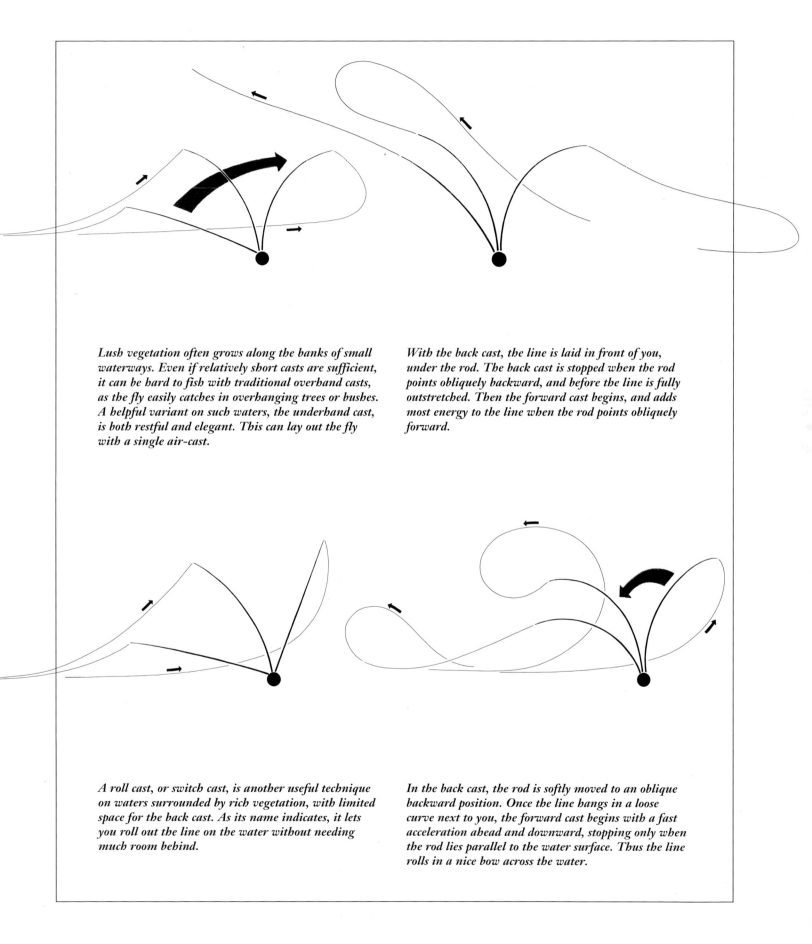

Lush vegetation often grows along the banks of small waterways. Even if relatively short casts are sufficient, it can be hard to fish with traditional overhand casts, as the fly easily catches in overhanging trees or bushes. A helpful variant on such waters, the underhand cast, is both restful and elegant. This can lay out the fly with a single air-cast.

With the back cast, the line is laid in front of you, under the rod. The back cast is stopped when the rod points obliquely backward, and before the line is fully outstretched. Then the forward cast begins, and adds most energy to the line when the rod points obliquely forward.

A roll cast, or switch cast, is another useful technique on waters surrounded by rich vegetation, with limited space for the back cast. As its name indicates, it lets you roll out the line on the water without needing much room behind.

In the back cast, the rod is softly moved to an oblique backward position. Once the line hangs in a loose curve next to you, the forward cast begins with a fast acceleration ahead and downward, stopping only when the rod lies parallel to the water surface. Thus the line rolls in a nice bow across the water.

present-day wet-fly fisherman prefers such a rod of at least 9 feet, and many of us go well over that figure.

A wet-fly rod should have a relatively slow, soft action. Flowing waters are often bordered by trees and bushes that make it difficult to fish with just the usual overhand cast. Instead, a wet-fly fisherman commonly uses underhand and roll casts, which are easier to perform with a softer rod.

But there are additional advantages to a soft, slow rod. A wet fly is supposed to sink through the water's surface rapidly. The fisherman can control this ability to some extent by tying his flies with an absorbent material, dressing them lightly, and giving them a suitable profile for penetrating the surface. However, the rod and casting technique are also important. A stiff fly-rod will cast the line in a fast curve that sprinkles water from the fly during the cast. A slower rod allows the fly to travel in a softer curve, retaining more water as it goes through the air. Thus the fly will sink more easily.

Types of water

Wet-fly fishing also occurs in still waters – as in Ireland from a drifting boat, in the English reservoirs, in Swedish put-and-take waters, and in the lakes of northern Scandinavia. But here, in general, flyfishing with streamers and diverse lures, pupae and nymphs has increasingly taken over the role of wet flies. So lake fishing will be discussed in connection with those types of flies.

Wet-fly fishing, then, is nowadays almost wholly reserved for fishing in running waters. Yet no two running waters are identical, and a wet-fly fishermen must adapt his strategy and technique to the stream section he is presently fishing on.

Fishing in streams and rivers

The characteristics of the water itself are exploited in wet-fly fishing to guide the fly toward the fish. Current speed, obstacles such as large stones, whirlpools, hollows, backwaters and other features affect the drift of insects on which the fish feed – and which, in turn, lead the fish to choose holding places. Fish can linger with less exertion in a current lee. But the insects are carried downstream in more concentrated current areas. Therefore, a good holding place combines lee and protection for the fish with an adequate flow of constantly passing food.

The wet-fly fisherman's strategy is to locate himself, in relation to the fish, so that he can cast his line and guide it to make the fly drift, with the underwater current, past the fish's lie at the same speed as the natural food. The line must float with minimum influence by current variations in the water. Otherwise the fly will immediately begin to "drag" in an unnatural manner, arousing the suspicion of fish and causing them to refuse it. From above the water, you would see instantly whether a dry fly is behaving naturally; but this is harder with a wet fly below the surface. The latter is also influenced not only by horizontal currents, but also by vertical ones – a further source of the difficulty, and the challenge, of wet-fly fishing.

Guiding the fly

An inexperienced wet-fly fisherman may regard variations of current between him and the fish as obstacles to his fishing. They can be bothersome and disturb the fly's drift by pulling the line with a different speed than what the fly should have. A skilled practitioner, though, watches for the opportunities provided by varying currents, as an aid to reaching the fish. He intentionally casts in ways that enable the current to guide his fly. He can slow down the line by mending upstream at the right moment. Sometimes he even mends downstream to speed up the line and fly. Both by mending, and by moving the rod tip, he can also trans-

An experienced flyfisherman can obtain much information from a particular sector of the current. Ability to "read the water" is very important for successful fishing in flowing waters. Bottom irregularities create eddies and backwaters, faster and slower flows, and "lanes" of movement. Often we speak of "feeding lines" where the food passes and fish tend to hold. It is thus an advantage to position yourself as closely as possible to such a line – although, of course, without standing right in it. Shown below in the illustration are locations of holding places in the current.

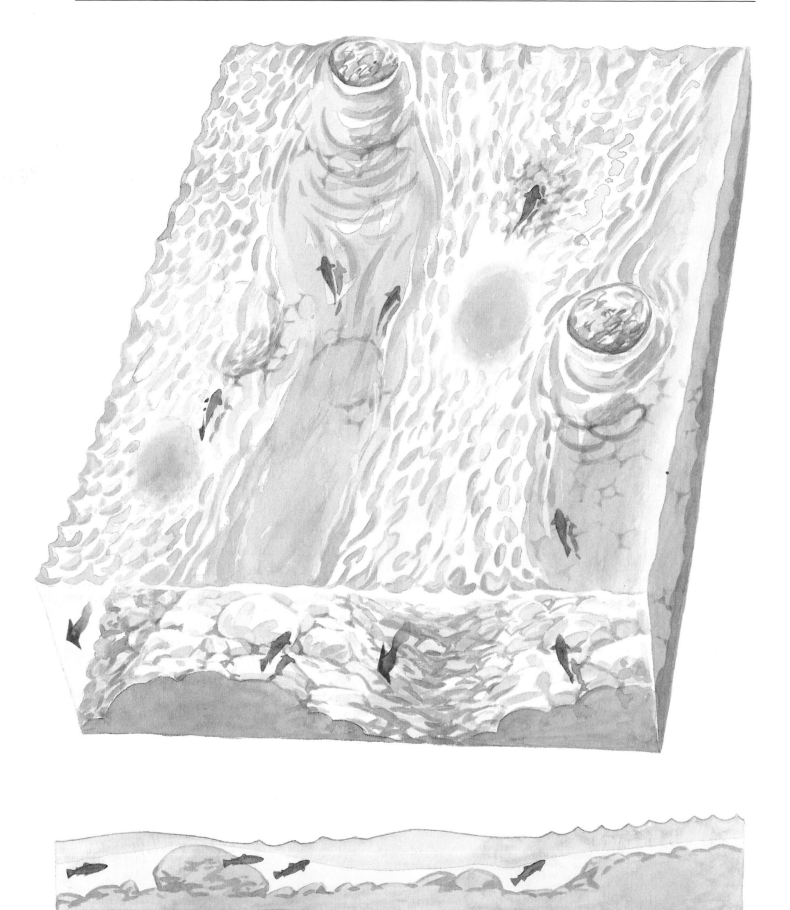

fer the line from one current to another, thus bringing the line to the areas of water he finds most interesting.

The idea that a line must float without any influence by the water is, of course, basically wrong. Obviously the line is under continual influence by the current and its variations. However, this idea shows what a wet-fly fisherman's goal should be. He has to handle the fly, leader and line in a manner that does not allow the current to "take command". The point is to let the current assist him in steering the fly with the right speed to the right place – where the fish are. It is thus a matter of exploiting the surface flows and braking, or speeding up, the line until you get into the "correct lane", just as when driving a car.

Where to cast from

Frequently the vegetation along a river bank prevents the wet-fly fisherman from selecting an ideal position for his casts. There may be bushes behind your back,

Fishing in small waterways can become rather crowded, calling for careful choice of your casting and fishing spot. Attention must be paid both to the likely holding places of fish, and to the opportunities for presenting your fly correctly.

as well as hanging branches at short distances both upstream and downstream from the fish's holding place. Trout are glad to stay in the shield of overhanging branches.

Sometimes you can wade out into the water and find a better spot from which to make your casts. But often you have to combine wading with a range of specialized casts – for instance, horizontally and perhaps with a left or right curve on the line. As already emphasized, a skilful wet-fly fisherman makes use of the currents between him and the fish, when guiding his line to the right place. A surface current of abnor-

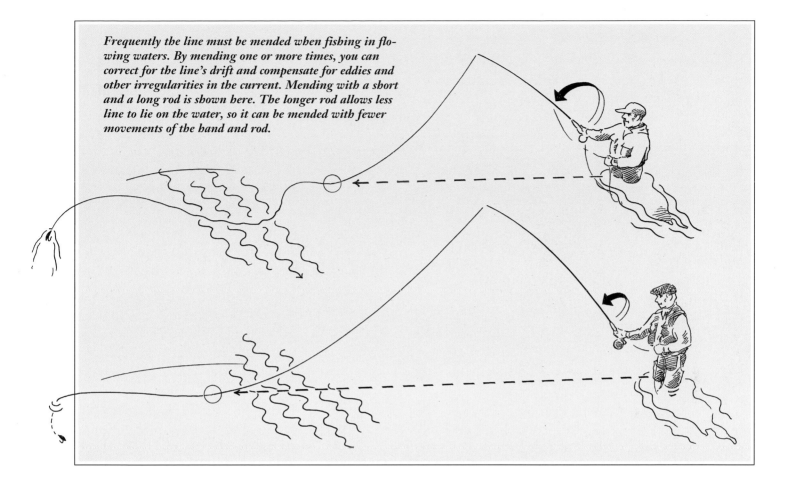

Frequently the line must be mended when fishing in flowing waters. By mending one or more times, you can correct for the line's drift and compensate for eddies and other irregularities in the current. Mending with a short and a long rod is shown here. The longer rod allows less line to lie on the water, so it can be mended with fewer movements of the hand and rod.

mal speed may sweep the line away or slow it down, depending on whether the surrounding water is more or less rapid. All of these variations can help the fisherman if he keeps moving the line in or out of the surface currents.

Compensating for fly drift

An example is the series of roll mendings – both upstream and downstream – which I learned during a fishing trip to Idaho some years ago. My guide demonstrated great skill in handling his floating line to obtain long, consistent drifts of the fly, with no disturbance by intermediate currents that threatened to pull his line away or brake it. Through sequences of rotating movements with the rod tip, he created "air rolls" along the line. These travelled out toward the end of the line, and allowed him to control his line curve even at a considerable distance. If a fast current of water promised to pull the line downstream, he rolled upstream; if another

swirl began to retard part of the line, he rolled this section downstream until it reached the rest of the line. By paying attention to the slightest changes in the water's character, he could correct the fly's drift down to the fish.

A longer rod makes it easier to control the line and the fly in such situations. If you wade out and fish with a short rod, a relatively great length of line will be lying on the water surface. With a long rod you can hold up more line, leaving less of it to be influenced by the surface currents. In addition, with a longer rod, you have more lever action and can get the rod tip to respond without moving your hand as much. This is very important as a rule, for instance when you use the above technique of roll-mending the line. It is also helpful when you want to lift the line over a troublesome current area, or guide the line into a suitable current edge that leads down toward the fish. But its main benefit is to increase the comfort of fishing, with limited hand movements instead of arm power.

The useful surface current

The surface current can be employed in further ways by a wet-fly fisherman. Since it is faster than the currents down in the water, it tends not only to pull the line sideways, but also to draw the fly upward. It therefore becomes an aid in raising the leader, and the fly, toward the surface. If you tighten up the line a little when the fly is at the fish's holding place, the faster surface current will give the fly an upward movement which is highly stimulating to the fish, and they often follow it to take the fly.

James E. Leisenring, frequently called the father of American wet-fly fishing, had a practice of actively encouraging this upward movement in order to provoke trout. He simply lifted his rod tip and took a light hold on the line, just when the fly reached the holding place. Then the surface current tighten up the leader, and the fly exhibited the attractive rising motion of a hatching insect. This technique has been named "Leisenring's lift".

in the cold water; so they are less willing to rise toward a fly that passes just above, or to one side of, their holding place. At such times you should fish a wet fly deep, and present it as close as possible to the fish's nose.

A sinking line, though, makes the fishing harder because it cannot be guided as easily with the rod on the water surface. Wet-fly fishing with a sinking line, therefore, should be limited to cold and deep waters with a strong but smooth current, where it is extremely difficult to get down to the fish with a floating line or sink-tip.

Using the roll cast's advantages

A sunken line may be heavy, and thus a burden on the rod when you lift to make a new cast. Here, too, the roll cast – so important in this kind of fishing – comes into play. For you can roll up the line on the surface in order to decrease its resistance by the water. Once this

Selecting a line

In shallow currents, a wet fly is normally fished with a floating line. But in deeper, stronger water it is preferable to use a sink-tip line. If you fish early in the season, when the water is cold and the fish stand deep, a sinking line can be the right choice. Since fish are cold-blooded animals, their metabolism becomes low

When making a roll cast with a heavy sunken line, it may be necessary to decrease the water resistance by first rolling up the line on the surface, before laying out the actual cast. This involves two casts, though normally done in a single movement.

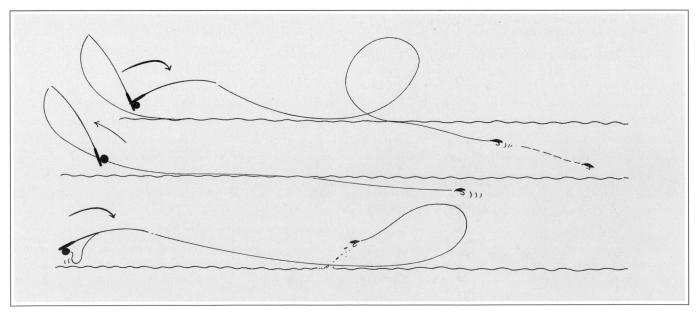

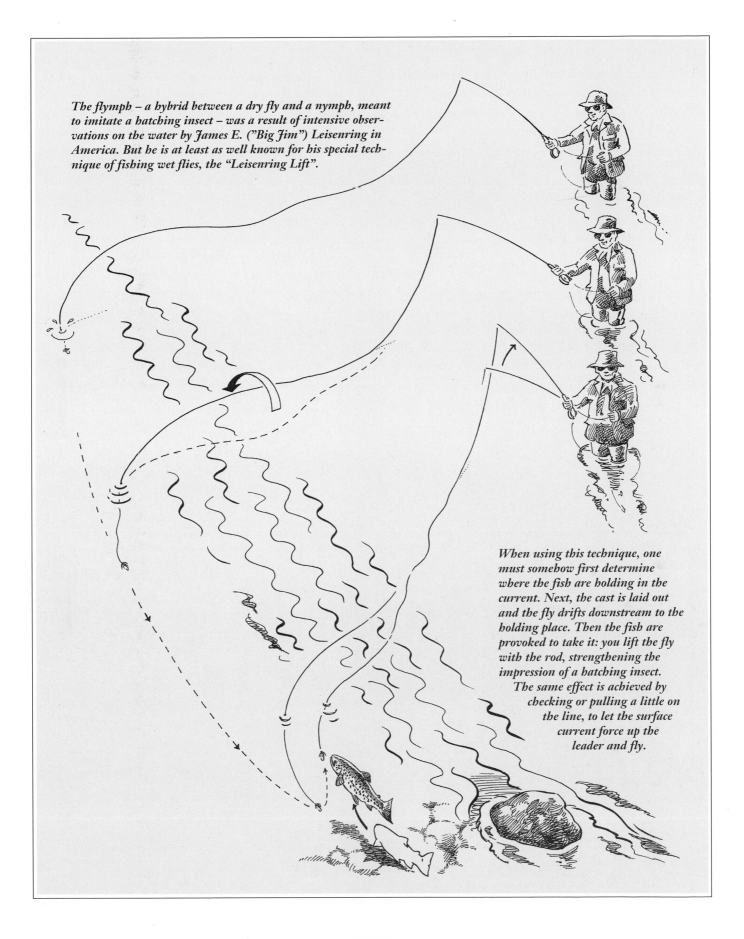

The flymph – a hybrid between a dry fly and a nymph, meant to imitate a hatching insect – was a result of intensive observations on the water by James E. ("Big Jim") Leisenring in America. But he is at least as well known for his special technique of fishing wet flies, the "Leisenring Lift".

When using this technique, one must somehow first determine where the fish are holding in the current. Next, the cast is laid out and the fly drifts downstream to the holding place. Then the fish are provoked to take it: you lift the fly with the rod, strengthening the impression of a hatching insect.
The same effect is achieved by checking or pulling a little on the line, to let the surface current force up the leader and fly.

is done, you can easily make a new cast, either the normal overhand type or another roll cast. But the angle should be out across the current, so that the fly lands in the right position to find its way down toward the fish.

Rolling up the fly on the surface, and subsequently casting, must be done as a continuous movement without any pause. It may seem strange when first attempted, but the technique is soon learned and will then provide a very useful cast – and not only for wet flies. It also works well when fishing with a floating line. Even the latter can be heavy to lift with a weak rod and a long line outside the top guide.

Aids to fishing at depth

Besides the range of available lines for bringing the fly down to a correct depth, you can weight the fly itself, by winding the hook shank with copper or lead wire.

At the same time, you shall avoid overdressing the fly. A powerful, bushy fly creates more resistance in the water and does not sink as readily.

In older fishing literature, it is often recommended that flies be tied sparsely. Many wet-fly fishermen through the years have discovered that an old, worn-out fly can fish better than a new one. The flies sold by sportfishing shops are generally too overdressed and bushy to fish well. There is good reason to suspect that they are tied to attract the fisherman rather than the fish. To be sure, flies tied with ample material seem to give you more for your money. Yet such a fly must be thoroughly soaked, for example by putting it in your mouth, before it can be made to sink at all – whereas a sparsely tied fly will sink at the first cast.

In flowing water, an oblique downstream cast is often used in order to give the fly time to sink to the right depth – where the fish are holding. Since the current is normally fastest at the surface, you should thus get the fly and leader underwater as quickly as possible.

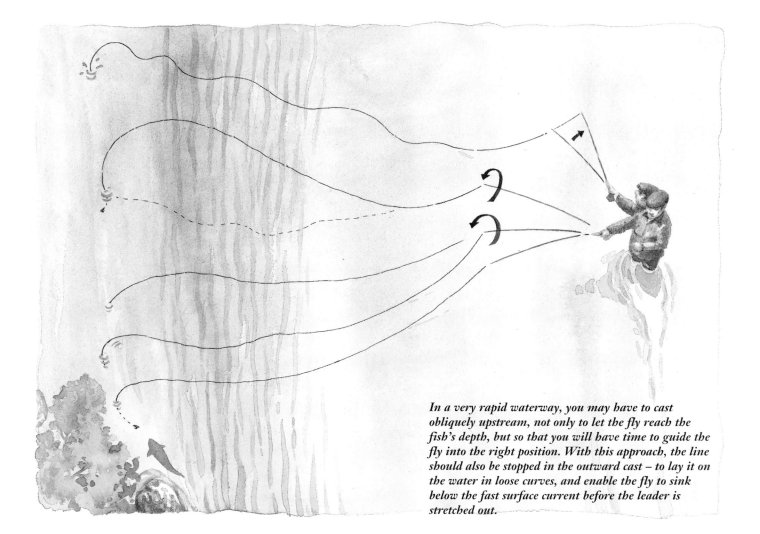

In a very rapid waterway, you may have to cast obliquely upstream, not only to let the fly reach the fish's depth, but so that you will have time to guide the fly into the right position. With this approach, the line should also be stopped in the outward cast – to lay it on the water in loose curves, and enable the fly to sink below the fast surface current before the leader is stretched out.

But you can also get the fly to sink faster by choosing a proper casting technique. As mentioned already, the current in a body of water is fastest at the surface, while at the bottom it is slowed down by stones and plants. Thus you have to make the leader and fly penetrate the surface current as quickly as possible. With a wet fly, the cast is usually laid obliquely over the water downstream. By instead casting across the current – or even somewhat upstream – and simultaneously stopping the rod so that the leader falls in loose curves, you will give the fly time to sink through the faster surface current before this stretches the leader. The fly will then be a good way under the surface before you need to mend the line and, using the rod, guide it toward the fish's holding place, where the fly can fish at the right level.

Outstretched casts

In recent years, ever more flyfishermen have acquired their first experience by put-and-take fishing on still waters. Lake flyfishing often calls for long casts, with a outstretched leader. The fish swim at some distance from the shore and can be hooked only if you have control over the cast.

A fisherman may transfer this technique with a outstretched line and leader to wet-fly fishing in flowing waters, without considering that the conditions in streams and rivers are entirely different. Here the stretched-cast strategy does not work, because the current instantly affects the line. If a stretched line is cast, its segments are pulled by the current at varying rates, curving it downstream and giving poor control of the fly. Consequently, a still-water fisherman has to rethink his technique when he switches to flowing water.

Many of us talk about "reading the water" in trying to figure out where the fish are. But it is at least as important to "read the water" in order to see how the currents move. The aim is to plan a correct strategy for how best to lay your cast and float the fly with minimum influence down to the fish's holding place.

Fishing environments

There are great differences between a Danish brook, an English chalk stream, an American spring creek, and a Scandinavian or Scottish river. Some waterways with swift stream are better suited than others to wet-fly fishing. So it is natural that this sport has become more solidly anchored with strong traditions in Scotland and Scandinavian countries.

The Scots are accustomed to using small, sparsely tied wet flies on the spider model. In Denmark the preference is for large, winged versions, while the rest of Scandinavia leans toward classics of the English variety. From these traditions, local types of flies with special colours have evolved.

Humus-coloured forest streams with poor visibility, for instance, demand more colourful flies than when fishing in crystal-clear mountain brooks. Similarly, a slow stream calls for wet flies tied with softer and

more lively material than does a rapid, violent river, where a wet fly made of stiffer stuff – such as cock hackle instead of hen hackle – works better.

Valuable experience

The designs of flies have been developed by generations of wet-fly fishermen through experience of conditions on their own local waters. But casting and fishing techniques have acquired distinctions as well. A fast, stony stream, where the trout find holding places in the current lees behind big boulders, invites "pocket fishing" at the most promising spots. In a flatland stream, the fish instead tend to stay in sections with insect-rich

Fish in a waterway select their holding places with care. When you "read" the water, a number of spots can thus be identified where trout are probably seeking protection, lee and food. Some typical holding places are: (1) just behind or alongside nutritious underwater vegetation, which offers both safety and shade; (2) in front of, or next to, cliffs and boulders; (3) before necks of water; (4) in deep and calm areas after a rapid stretch; (5) below overhanging trees, hollowed-out banks, and big roots.

vegetation, behind bridge pillars, in deeply eroded areas by the banks, or in the characteristic Danish "swing" where a stream turns and the water has dug a deeper outside bend.

The watchfulness and behaviour of fish are also different in each kind of waterway. Fish are much more shy and easily frightened in a stream with low, clear water than in a deep river. The fish in a small stream often stand beneath the cover of hanging bushes, or under a "roof" of turbulent foamy water – and sometimes they only relax their attentiveness under the cloak of the dark hours.

Approaching the water

The senses used by animals in order to survive depend on their species. Predatory birds have a fantastic ability to resolve the image on their retinas, and dogs are far better than humans at following a scent. We ourselves rely mainly on hearing and vision, but easily forget that the fish also have senses which we lack. As we get close to a stream, many of us commit a serious mistake that is worth pointing out.

A waterway is surrounded by ground whose character may vary widely, from bare virgin rock to a bog. Our manner of approaching the water, therefore, may have a great influence. The fish – due to their lateral line, an organ sensitive to vibrations running along their body sides, with branches along the gill covers and head – can pick up disturbances in the water which are created by our steps and movements on land. So we cannot prevent the fish from detecting us by simply keeping a low profile: we should move slowly and cautiously, to avoid sending vibrations into the water and disclosing our presence. Often a period of quiet waiting by the waterside will calm down the fish again, before we begin fishing. A disturbed fish can never be coaxed to take the fly.

Reading with care

In other words, get ready to fish as you approach the water. A discreet arrival is an essential starting-point for the wet-fly fisherman's strategy. Next you have to "read", or study, the water and judge where the fish are likely to be. In downstream wet-fly fishing, the first casts are normally toward places of interest that

As is well known, fish that have been frightened will refuse to take even the best-presented fly for a while – perhaps half an hour or more. A wise strategy is therefore to approach the water cautiously in a low posture, and wait a bit before starting to fish. This pause should be utilized by reading the water, trying to figure out the fish's holding places, studying the insect life and making other observations of tactical value.

lie closest to your own bank. Only after that you should cast farther out. Otherwise the line might fall over a fish which is relatively nearby. A line that passes over a fish will very probably frighten it, and make it refuse to take flies. Again, fish in waterways differ from those in still waters. Lake fish can swim away if they are startled, and continue eating at a distance – whereas a fish in a current has both a chosen holding place for eating and a nearby hiding place. If it is frightened there, it will leave for the hiding place, or else move down to the bottom and eat nothing.

When you have found a suitable fish, you can be fairly sure that it will stay in its holding place as long as it is not startled. So you have a reasonable time to organize your fishing strategy. Calmly inspect the current formations between the fish and the chosen casting spot. You have to "read" the water anew, but the aim is now to decide how your line can be cast in order to float downstream with as little influence by the water as possible.

Exploiting the currents

Parts of the surface that go much faster than the surrounding water will change the line's drift, and this negative effect must be kept to a minimum. It is also necessary to calculate how far in front of the fish you must cast the fly itself, so that it can sink to the fish's level before the cast is fished out.

Often you find that the currents can indeed be exploited to do the job, for instance by changing the line's drift or by sweeping it into a flow that passes just by the holding place. More difficult, though, is to judge the underwater currents in vertical directions, which continually threaten to ruin the fly's drift. Since these currents are invisible, your only clues are slight movements at the point where the line end or the leader vanishes down into the water.

A great challenge

The fact that you cannot see the fly is not merely a drawback of wet-fly fishing in comparison to its dry-fly counterpart. The other side of the coin is an equal, or even greater, excitement for the flyfisherman who knows how to appreciate this extraordinary sport. Unfortunately, wet-fly fishing has suffered some scorn in the recent past, while ever more people have been attracted to fishing with dry flies, nymphs and pupae. Fishing with a wet fly is by no means an "undeveloped" form of fishing, and it calls for the right kind of enthusiast – as the newcomer will very soon discover!

Wet-fly fishermen in well-defined localities gradually learn the special conditions that prevail on their waters, and how the fishing varies with the seasons. They also know which flies fish best in their currents. So they are the ones who harvest the finest triumphs when fishing with wet flies.

How fish take flies

In wet-fly fishing, you seldom see the fish take the fly. Yet many adept practitioners develop a sort of intuition that enables them to deduce what is happening under the water, and makes it easier to hook the fish.

If the water is not too turbulent, there may be a chance to notice whether the leader is pulled downward or sideways. And in quite shallow water, or with

a fly being fished close to the surface, you can sometimes have a glimpse just under the surface when a fish takes. Generally, however, your sole information comes through the rod and line, by feeling how the line tightens up and you make a counterstrike to hook the fish.

No rule without exceptions

A wet fly is normally taken with calmer movements than a dry fly. This is not unexpected, since the current down near the fish's holding place is slower than the surface current transporting a dry fly. The fish has more time to take a wet fly, and need not make such a rapid rush as when it rises for a dry fly. But here too – as with all fishing – there are exceptions to prove the rule. Luckily a wet-fly fisherman never quite completes his training: every fishing trip brings further lessons and surprises...

Occasionally, for example, a fish may leave the holding place and follow a wet fly far downstream with interest, finally taking it in a frenzy just as it is about to swing out of the current and disappear.

Some wet flies also take advantage of the fish's territorial habits by provoking a strike. These are the fantasy flies that do not resemble the fish's natural food in any way. They may have strong colours and excessive dimensions, which a fish regards as a threat to its own domain. Such a fly has to be got rid of – and the strike is predictably violent. The fish may even follow the fly even outside its territory.

Still, the basic principle is that you first feel only a tug on the line. At times it is an extremely weak response, and the wet-fly fisherman may at first miss a lot of fish before he learns to interpret their signals. But once he is learning, he may well have his share of sport!

Wet-fly fishing demands great concentration and presence of mind. The signal that a fish has taken the fly is often very discreet, but you have to notice it and react as soon as possible. The slightest sign of abnormal movement by the leader or line tip in the current can mean that a trout is hooked.

Nymph
Fishing

While our fishing flies were originally meant to imitate different natural flies and other water insects, wet-fly fishermen soon noticed that certain colours, or combinations of these, were more effective than the rest. So they began to add flagrant details, such as a red tail, and many wet flies evolved into pure fantasy flies with no real resemblance to natural models. Besides, there was a tendency to follow tradition – and the fact that fantasy flies, after all, did catch fish. Nonetheless, some flyfishermen started investigating the stomach contents of their catches, and found that the food organisms on the fish's menu varied with the time of year. A further advance was the establishment of a simple system by determining the species of the most common insects.

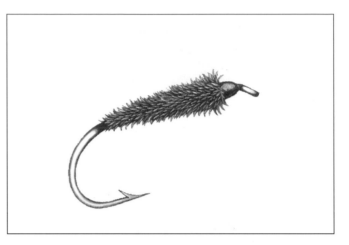

The peacock nymph, one of the first nymphs described in flyfishing literature, is quite simple: it consists of a hook wound with a peacock herl.

Pure imitation flies

The interest grew in creating new imitation flies to be fished underwater, and it was strengthened as ever more flyfishermen gained a knowledge of entomology. True correspondence with the underwater stages of living insects was aimed for. This pioneering movement turned away from the traditional wet-fly fishing, which was thought to have become stereotyped and no longer suited to present requirements. Of course, the old wet flies did not completely disappear, and many patterns are still fished today with success.

Nymph fishing was born out of these fresh efforts. As mentioned already, the first fishing flies were imitations of particular insects at each month of the year. For example, as early as the 1600s, Charles Cotton described a simple fly that was just "a peacock's whirl without wings" – in other words, a peacock herl wrapped around the hook shank. This might have been the oldest description of a nymph in flyfishing literature. However, judging by his account, the "nymph" was

probably a little green larva which had tumbled down from a tree on the bank, not a nymph in the strictly entomological sense that we need to adopt.

A comprehensive term

Rather wrongly, though, nymph fishing has gradually been taken to include almost all fishing with imitation flies underwater, and sometimes even with insects which have no nymph stage. Previously, we learned that fly eggs develop into larvae, but that all of these need not become nymphs: they turn into pupae if they belong to the insect groups with complete metamorphosis. The true nymphs are found among mayflies, stoneflies, and dragonflies – such as the damselflies – whereas caddis flies and midges, for instance, never become nymphs, as their larvae undergo pupation on the way to hatching as winged adults.

For convenience, we may continue to speak of nymph fishing as a collective term when fishing our imitation flies underwater. Still, it is essential for a nymph fisherman who bases his or her sport on ento-

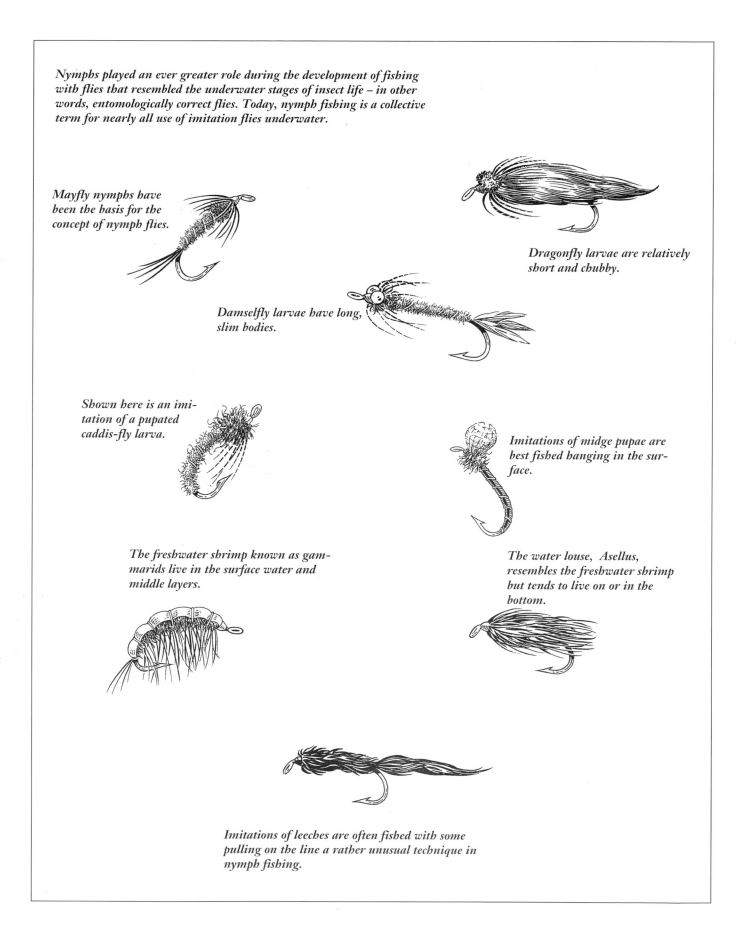

Nymphs played an ever greater role during the development of fishing with flies that resembled the underwater stages of insect life – in other words, entomologically correct flies. Today, nymph fishing is a collective term for nearly all use of imitation flies underwater.

Mayfly nymphs have been the basis for the concept of nymph flies.

Dragonfly larvae are relatively short and chubby.

Damselfly larvae have long, slim bodies.

Shown here is an imitation of a pupated caddis-fly larva.

Imitations of midge pupae are best fished hanging in the surface.

The freshwater shrimp known as gammarids live in the surface water and middle layers.

The water louse, Asellus, resembles the freshwater shrimp but tends to live on or in the bottom.

Imitations of leeches are often fished with some pulling on the line a rather unusual technique in nymph fishing.

As in all flyfishing, it is important to choose your fly with regard to the water you are fishing in. Calm parts of flowing waters, as shown here (left), often have an insect fauna similar to that in lakes and other still waters. Only by looking at the water surface can you tell what lies beneath it.

mology to make proper distinctions between larvae, pupae and nymphs, as well as to learn the different insects' life cycles and stages of development, in order to fully benefit from the sport.

The right nymph in the right environment

Each kind of water environment gives rise to its own living conditions. The nutritious English chalk streams, for example, are a good habitat for species of mayfly to thrive in. Thus it was natural that the love of fishing with imitations of mayfly nymphs was initiated and refined in England. Elsewhere, as in Scandinavia which has other types of freestone rivers and less chalky waters, flyfishermen instead concentrated on imitations of caddis-fly pupae, since these are a more prominent group of insects in local terms.

Further insects play a key role for the lake flyfisherman. This is illustrated by imitations of damselfly nymphs and midge pupae. Popular, too, are trout food organisms that, from an entomological viewpoint, are neither nymphs nor pupae, such as diverse species of water-living bugs and crustaceans.

The concept of nymph fishing, then, can be extended to a host of imitation flies. But an entomologically interested flyfisherman should try to distinguish among the underwater forms of insects, allowing nymphs to be nymphs and pupae to be pupae – in addition to recognizing that other water-living creatures do not belong to those groups – even if he or she occasionally places all underwater fishing with imitation flies in the category of nymph fishing.

(Left) The insect life is always adapted to its environment. When fishing in flowing waters, one must take account of the current strength in order to be sure of how the nymphs look. In a fast stretch, the nymphs are flat and have powerful legs (far left) to avoid being pulled by the current. But in quiet areas of the same waterway, with conditions resembling still waters, swimming nymphs with developed gills are common.

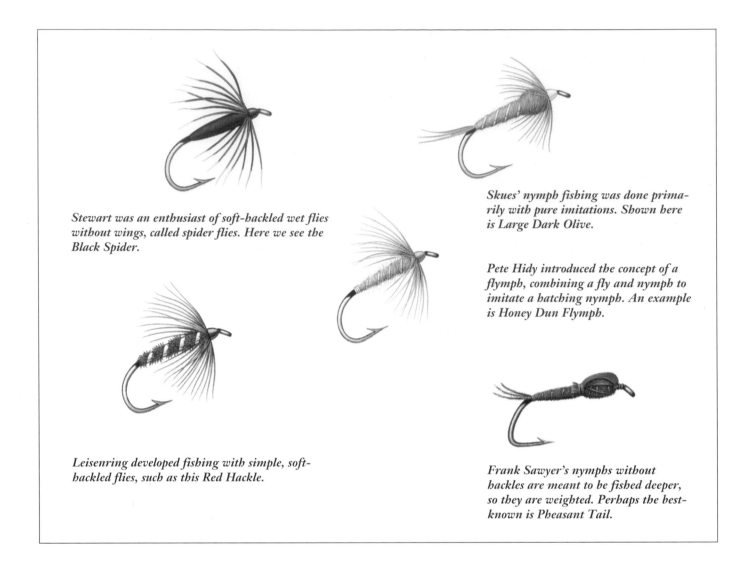

Stewart was an enthusiast of soft-hackled wet flies without wings, called spider flies. Here we see the Black Spider.

Skues' nymph fishing was done primarily with pure imitations. Shown here is Large Dark Olive.

Pete Hidy introduced the concept of a flymph, combining a fly and nymph to imitate a hatching nymph. An example is Honey Dun Flymph.

Leisenring developed fishing with simple, soft-backled flies, such as this Red Hackle.

Frank Sawyer's nymphs without hackles are meant to be fished deeper, so they are weighted. Perhaps the best-known is Pheasant Tail.

Stewart and Skues

In 1857 the Scottish flyfisherman W. C. Stewart published his little book "The Practical Angler", which was to attract wide attention. He advocated fishing with lightly dressed "spider" flies. As soft-hackled wet flies without wings, they were good all-round nymph imitations. He emphasized that they should have very sparse dressing, thin tapered bodies, and a lively soft hackle – characteristics in contrast to traditional wet flies.

Stewart's flies and fishing technique clearly indicated a trend towards the nymph fishing we know today. He thereby paved the way for the father of English nymph fishing, G. E. M. Skues. This authority based his sport on pure imitations of the nymphs he found in his own waters, and tied them to agree in detail with their natural prototypes.

A careful craft of imitation

While Stewart's flies were rather simple, with a relatively long hackle, Skues provided nymphs with tails and a marked thorax and much shorter hackle. The two authors' books also reveal a fundamental difference: Stewart regarded his flies as "general imitations" and was most concerned with their presentation, whereas Skues had studied live nymphs closely and acquired the technique of pure imitation already at the tying stage, as well as carefully choosing nuances of colour in his material.

On the other hand, Stewart and Skues agreed that their fishing ought to be based on entomology and correct presentation. The dissimilarities between their flies is mostly a reflection of those between Stewart's fast-flowing, less nutritious Scottish running waters –

in which the fish have less time or energy to be fastidious – and Skues' slow-moving, glassy, food-rich southern English chalk streams.

Leisenring, Hidy and Sawyer

Skues corresponded with the American wet-fly fisherman James E. Leisenring, who had independently arrived at a method of fishing with simple, soft-hackled wet flies on his side of the Atlantic. It was from their common experience that modern nymph fishing arose, and both were to have followers and build traditions. In America, Leisenring's friend and disciple Pete Hidy invented the concept of a flymph, combining a "fly" and "nymph", to imitate a hatching nymph (or caddis-fly pupa) that was struggling in the water surface to escape from its skin and become a winged insect.

In England, Frank Sawyer introduced weighted nymphs, to be fished deeper down in the water's middle levels. Hidy's flymphs have dubbed bodies enclosing tiny air bubbles, which enable them to "mimic" the air layer under a nymph's or pupa's skin, yielding the silvery appearance that we mentioned earlier. A flymph also has a soft front hackle to create the illusion of half-developed wings and struggling insect legs.

The selection of material and the tying technique give a flymph some buoyancy, for a hatching insect must be fished in the surface. Besides, many flies either fail to hatch fully, or die in this state without taking wings. These "stillborns", too, can be imitated with a flymph. Despite its simplicity, therefore, a flymph is a well-planned fly.

Swimming nymphs

Frank Sawyer's nymphs are designed for quite different fishing, deeper in the water. Therefore, they are weighted with copper wire and have no hackle. A hackle would increase their volume and, consequently, their water-resistance and tendency to sink. Moreover, such nymphs are supposed to imitate various species of swimming nymphs which, according to Sawyer's studies, keep their legs folded under the body when swimming.

Hence, the weighted nymph with a slim body and marked thorax, but lacking a hackle, fits Sawyer's recipe – as regards both the ability to sink quickly to the right depth, and the requirement that an imitation's

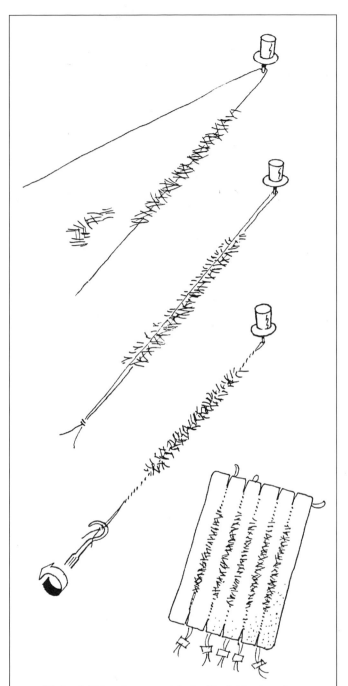

If the dubbing is spun with double-laid tying thread or silk, it will give both nymphs and flymphs a much livelier body. The result is a "mimicry" effect: many air bubbles are formed on the body, enhancing the fly's resemblance to a real insect.

appearance should be characteristic of the real models and their way of swimming. Here, once again, tying techniques and fishing techniques have gone hand in hand.

Many other flyfishermen around the world have continued to discover new types of nymph, larva and pupa imitations for the underwater stages of insect species. Examples are midge pupae, the larvae and pupae of caddis flies, and the nymphs of stoneflies and damselflies – as well as the underwater bugs and crustaceans which we sometimes include in nymph fishing.

Fantasy nymphs

A nymph may also turn into a "general fly" when it becomes popular outside the region where it originated. Such is the matter with the "Montana nymph" in America, which imitates a large stonefly nymph. This can no longer be considered an imitation fly when fished elsewhere in the world, since the corresponding insect does not exist there. In addition, stonefly nymphs are bottom-living insects that creep among the stones, while in stillwater fishing they are usually fished out in the open free waters. A lack of entomological insight – plus practical experience of the Montana nymph's good catching qualities – has thus allowed it to pass from an imitation fly to being a pure fantasy nymph.

Evidently the concept of nymph fishing is quite flexible, and we face a risk of seeing our nymphs and pupae meet the same fate as the old wet flies. It has already been noted how many wet flies ceased to imitate specific, natural insects and survived as fantasy flies without much similarity to their prototypes.

Nymph-fishing technique

In river fishing, the method of fishing nymphs is derived mainly from wet-fly fishing. One lets the nymph drift freely underwater at the depth where one expects the fish to hunt. But the process is not as stereotyped as wet-fly fishing with a downstream cast, because one varies the cast both downstream and upstream in order to make the nymph sink to different depths. Further, one chooses the kind of nymph according to the desired depth. A weighted Sawyer nymph, with its

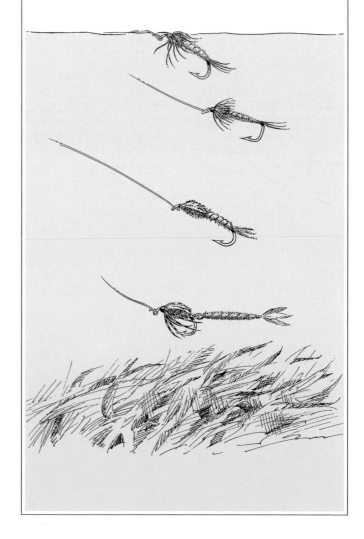

Since we are imitating nymphs that live at different depths, there are some simple rules to be followed when choosing the fly, leader and line. The illustration shows at what depths the various types of nymph should be fished: for a flymph, imitating a hatching insect, only 1-2 cm below the surface; for the Skues type of nymph, in the upper part of the middle water layer; for the Sawyer nymph, somewhat deeper. At the bottom are fished deep-sinking nymphs, such as this damselfly imitation. The most common way of making a nymph fish at the desired depth is, of course, to weight it.

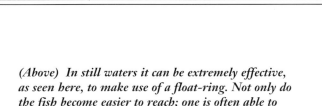

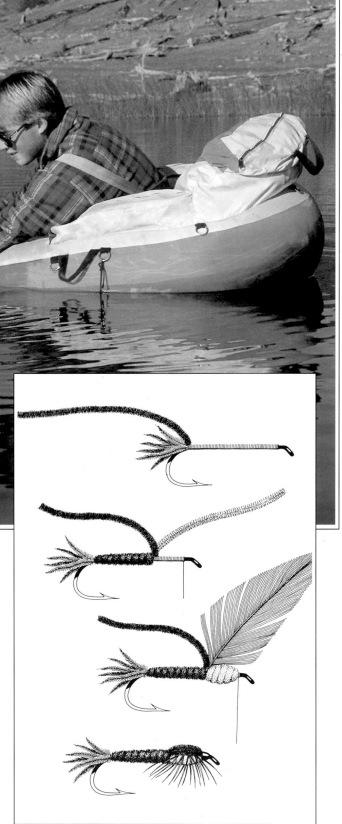

(Above) In still waters it can be extremely effective, as seen here, to make use of a float-ring. Not only do the fish become easier to reach; one is often able to sneak up on them without causing terror.

 (Right) Several types of nymphs are attractive to trout even if the natural prototypes do not occur in the water at hand. Among the best-known such "all-round nymphs" is Montana, which comes in colour variants and has harvested with success around the world. It is both easy to vary and simple to tie.

slender profile, is bound to sink faster than a Skues nymph or a Hidy flymph, since these have hackles and resist the water more.

Just as in wet-fly fishing, the casting technique and presentation are extremely important. Indeed, nymph fishing calls for even greater imagination and variety. For instance, today's rapid-action fly rods, and the tendency to cast with a narrow line curve, dry out the fly more than a soft cast with a more open line curve, which does not shake as much water out of the fly. Then the nymph is wetter when it hits the water, breaks more easily through the surface, and sinks faster.

Reaching the correct depth

A long leader that is not completely outstretched but laid in lazy curves, as described previously for fishing in flowing water, will give the nymph more time to sink before the leader is stretched out by the current, which is always strongest at the surface. Together with an upstream cast, a softer technique and a slack leader, one can thus coax the nymph to reach a correct depth

Since fish in flowing waters usually wait at their holding places for food to drift past, you must give a drifting nymph time to sink to the fish's depth – by placing it as far upstream as possible, without hampering your presentation. To see when the trout takes the nymph, you should keep watching for the leader to move sideways or suddenly dive.

– whereas casting with a narrow line loop with a stretched leader and oblique downstream cast will force the nymph to fish superficially.

A lot of flyfishermen seem to believe that weighting the nymph, or else greasing the leader, is what determines the depth at which the nymph will fish. This is presumably because flyfishermen increasingly get their training on still waters; but there are far more, and quite important, ways to influence the nymph's descent in flowing waters. Once the faster surface water has taken hold of the line and leader, your chances of controlling this descent are very limited. The only recourse is then to mend the line and prevent a downstream curve, which pull the leader and nymph up toward the surface.

Thin leaders

Normally a nymph fisherman uses a leader tip as long and thin as the circumstances allow – partly to avoid scaring the fish, but chiefly to make the little nymph move as realistically as possible. The choice of leader diameter may also be based on the fact that a thinner diameter creates less water resistance, helping the nymph to sink quickly.

It is worth stressing here that the nymph fisherman should not forget how much faster the water flows at the surface. The nymph must break through this to reach the slower water – and the fish. A different situation applies to still waters, in which one can ignore the current's effect on the nymph, line and leader.

Points to remember

There are other relevant contrasts between flowing and still waters. While the water in a river or stream transports food to the fish, in a lake the fish have to swim about and hunt prey. In the case of nymph fishing, this means we can make use of the current to fish out the cast, whereas in a lake we must retrieve the nymph with short hand twists to give it a lively movement. We also choose different materials for flies, depending on which kind of fishing is done. A lake flyfisherman often ties with marabou fibres or similar soft materials, as they allow the nymph to move more freely and vitally.

Besides these properties, a nymph should certainly have the right entomological appearance – at least within fairly narrow limits of form, colour and size. But we need not expect the fish to count the number of tails on a nymph, and refuse it if there are more or less than three!

Pupa fishing

During recent decades, fishing with caddis and midge pupae has acquired a central role. The interest in pupa fishing is due partly to the widespread decline in mayflies because of pollution, caddis flies and midges being relatively tolerant. Another reason is that the latter hatch for a longer time in the season, so that their pupae have become ever more appealing to the entomologically oriented flyfisherman.

With improved communications, too, increasing numbers of flyfishermen travel to northerly waters, where the species are fewer but the abundance of caddis flies and midges is amazing. The luminous summers of "midnight sun" yield high production for a short, intensive period – unlike the longer, slower seasonal cycle of southern waters. Hence, it is in the north that a flyfisherman can experience the spectacular pupa hatches which have made this type of fishing so popular.

The excitement of pupa fishing is greatest in connection with large hatches. Even if there are many

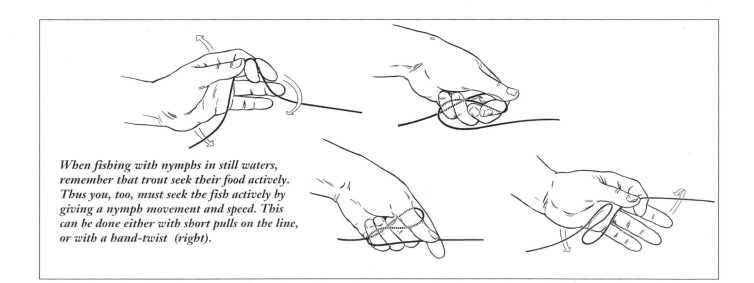

When fishing with nymphs in still waters, remember that trout seek their food actively. Thus you, too, must seek the fish actively by giving a nymph movement and speed. This can be done either with short pulls on the line, or with a hand-twist (right).

winged insects on the water or above it, our focus should be on the pupae. For the fish find these easier to catch and, faced with such a surplus, concentrate entirely on what is happening in, or right below, the surface.

Caddis-fly larvae and pupae

One of the most catching flies ever composed, the Gold Ribbed Hare's Ear, consists in its simplest form of a body with hare-ear dubbing and a gold rib – just a little "sausage" on which, perhaps, some strands are picked out with the dubbing needle. Its superb performance is easy to understand, as it represents a long series of different caddis-fly larvae and pupae. Moreover, it demonstrates that a wealth details, whether of wing rudiments or legs or antennae, does not necessarily make an imitation any better in the fish's eyes.

Another excellent floating caddis-fly pupa is the Superpuppa, invented by Lennart Bergqvist. Its two-coloured body, with a darker thorax, has a Palmer hackle that is clipped both on top and below, so that it can float upon the water when greased.

Fishing in the surface

Also worth mentioning, among caddis-fly pupa imitations, is a flymph with an olive-green dubbed abdomen, a thorax of hare-ear wool, and a sparse partridge hackle. It, too, is meant to be fished in or slightly below the water surface. Nor should your fly-box fail to include Gary LaFontaine's Sparkling Pupa. This has a dubbed underbody, with Antron yarn fibres folded over it to form a "bag" that resembles the hatching caddis-fly pupa's air-filled, silvery abdomen. The thorax is dubbed with darker fibres – and a fully floating, hatching variant has a sparse wing of elk hair as well.

Otherwise, a traditional caddis-fly pupa imitation is tied with a relatively thick, dubbed abdomen in beige, olive green or darker green, and a dark-brown thorax. Sometimes it is given wing-cases, lying along the thorax sides, and more seldom a few sparse hackle strands to suggest the pupa's long paddle-legs.

Emergent Sparkle Pupa

Green caddis-fly flymph

Gold Ribbed Hare's Ear

Borsten.

Gill-ribbed larvae

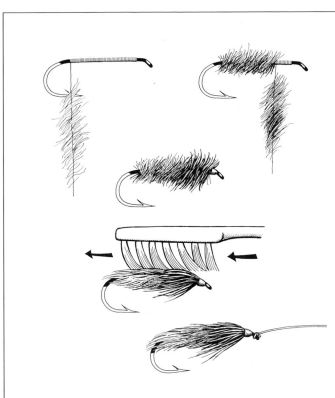

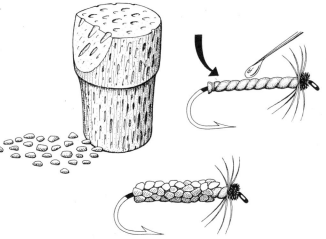

Superpupa is another excellent imitation of caddis-fly pupae, made in numerous colour variants. The fly is tied with thick poly dubbing or natural underwool, and should have a shaggy body. The body hackle, wound over the body's front and back, is trimmed above and below the hook shaft. It floats if greased, but otherwise sinks slowly.

Nalle Puh (Winnie the Pooh) is a Finnish fly created by Simon Lumme, originally tied with bear fur. It also comes in a pupa version, tied on hook size 10-16, usually with a rear body of dirty-orange or olive-green dubbing, and a front body of thick dubbing from hare's ear. The whole body must be ample so that, while fishing, the fly will hold tiny glittering air bubbles, imitating a gas-filled pupa.

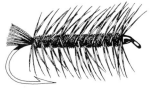

There are several good imitations of case-worms, the "house-building" stage of caddis-fly larvae. An American fly that superbly imitates case-worms which build their houses of plant pieces is Wooly Worm. With chenille – available in many colours – the right case-worm profile is first built up. Then grizzle or black cock hackle is wound all along the body. The fly should be weighted and fished with short pulls on the line.

Caddis-fly larvae that build their "houses" of sand and gravel are harder to imitate. But a good method is to thread a piece of valve rubber (about 2 cm long) over a long-shafted hook, brush it with a layer of glue, and roll it in cork crumbs torn or filed from a bottle-cork. The head and legs are imitated by winding it with a peacock herl and one or two turns of black cock hackle.

Midge pupae

A hatching midge pupa has a long, slim, clearly segmented abdomen, and a marked breast segment with short wing rudiments lying parallel along the sides. Its details, however, are small and less important to imitate. The general impression of the elongated body and conspicuous thorax is enough. A good complement is a white yarn tuft on top of the head, which becomes very striking when the pupa hangs in the water's surface film and the fish see it against the light from above. This tuft also contributes to the pupa's buoyancy, which can be further improved with a single turn of soft hen hackle. Moreover, the white tuft helps a flyfisherman to locate the pupa on the water – often a difficult task, as it hangs so low in the surface film.

The live pupa wriggles back and forth to free its long body from the pupal skin. But at intervals it hangs motionless, resting in the surface, and this is what we imitate. Our fly is thus fished almost without moving, as it waits for a fish to take it. Considerable patience may be needed when the hatches are massive and your own pupa has to compete with thousands of real ones.

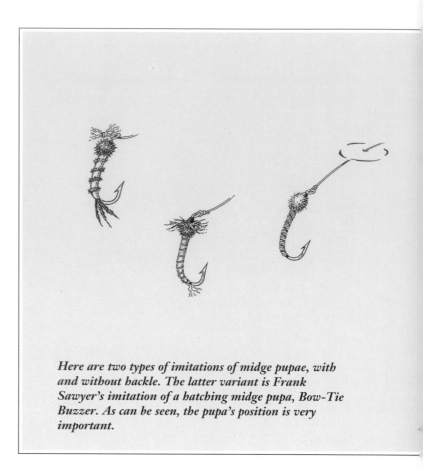

Here are two types of imitations of midge pupae, with and without hackle. The latter variant is Frank Sawyer's imitation of a hatching midge pupa, Bow-Tie Buzzer. As can be seen, the pupa's position is very important.

Trout eating midge pupae often move slowly and lazily, tending to swim in a definite direction.

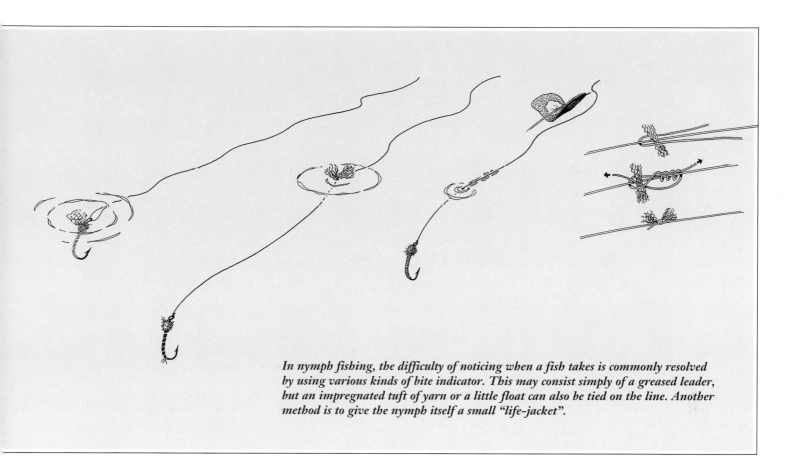

In nymph fishing, the difficulty of noticing when a fish takes is commonly resolved by using various kinds of bite indicator. This may consist simply of a greased leader, but an impregnated tuft of yarn or a little float can also be tied on the line. Another method is to give the nymph itself a small "life-jacket".

Frank Sawyer composed an interesting variant of a hatching midge pupa, the Bow-Tie Buzzer. He pulled the leader through the hook eye and fastened it with a knot in a piece of white yarn. This was clipped short to stop up in the hook eye, at the same time imitating the pupa's gill tufts. The knot's advantage is that the pupa hangs completely free on the leader.

Short-range fishing

In recent years, the development of light carbon-fibre rods for ever lower AFTM classes has increased the popularity of fishing with small, delicate nymphs at short range with rods of class 3 or 4. Nymph fishing is essentially suited to rather short casts, which allow the nymph fisherman to keep a visual watch on the point where the leader breaks the water and disappears under the surface. Unlike downstream wet-fly fishing, in which one tends to feel the fish take instead of

seeing it, the nymph fisherman is thus more dependent on seeing how the greased leader hesitates or is pulled sideways, indicating that a fish has taken the nymph in its mouth.

A modern carbon-fibre rod built for short casts, with a very light line, therefore gives a whole new dimension in nymph fishing, compared to heavier and more traditional equipment. By using a fairly soft rod with full action, one can cast easier with more open line loops. This prevents shaking more water than necessary out of the nymph, so that it can sink faster. For the same reason, needless blind casts should be avoided: the goal is a casting technique that gets the nymph out on the water again quickly. Such a rod is also ideal for roll casts, which are wasted by many of today's flyfishermen, but are particularly useful in nymph fishing.

Naturally, the casting technique depends on the type of nymph or pupa which is knotted to the leader. A weighted Sawyer nymph, tied with pheasant-tail

In small, turbulent waters, you can use a somewhat heavier line than what the rod is classed for. By fishing with a bite indicator, the fly's location is relatively easy to see.

fibres, cannot and need not hold as much water as a Skues nymph. In the case of a Hidy flymph, it may even be an advantage to shake out some water so that the fly will float right in the surface – or so as to create a mimicry effect.

In sum, any nymph is a combination of the materials it is tied with and the way it is fished in the water, a fact the experienced nymph fisherman never loses sight of.

Good help from a strike indicator

While short-range fishing with a light rod and line is especially handy in small waterways, or in lake fishing near shores, there are definitely occasions when ordi-

nary equipment of class 5-6 is more suitable, not least for fishing in still waters. A typical situation is that the fish take midge pupae at a fair distance from the shore. Here a longer rod in a somewhat higher AFTM class makes it easier to lift the longer line and cast again.

However, with such casting lengths, say of 20 metres or more, it is virtually impossible to follow the leader's movement by eye – regardless of whether you grease your leader or not. When fishing with a midge

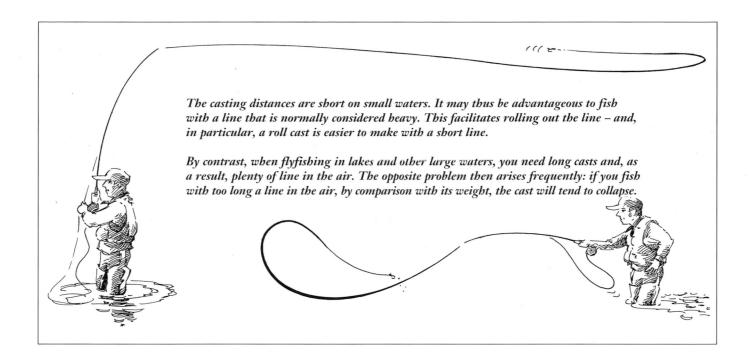

The casting distances are short on small waters. It may thus be advantageous to fish with a line that is normally considered heavy. This facilitates rolling out the line – and, in particular, a roll cast is easier to make with a short line.

By contrast, when flyfishing in lakes and other large waters, you need long casts and, as a result, plenty of line in the air. The opposite problem then arises frequently: if you fish with too long a line in the air, by comparison with its weight, the cast will tend to collapse.

pupa that hangs in the surface film, you can watch the fish taking it; but when fishing slightly below the surface, a strike indicator can be a valuable aid with long casts.

Some nymph fishermen also like to use a strike indicator in fast and turbulent water, where the leader may be hard to follow exactly by eye on the swirling surface. Personally, though, I find it better to rely mainly on the signals from the leader and line to my fingers. Thus, I depend more on what I feel than on what I see – as well as on my intuition, to some extent. For the water's influence on the leader is so great that a strike indicator usually gives a "false alarm" as often as a true sign that a fish has taken the nymph in its mouth.

A strike indicator may consist of a small, elongated float on the leader, or a colourful piece of yarn tied around it, and greased for good buoyancy.

Entomological flyfishing

In which environments, and at which times, we can fish with various nymphs and pupae has been explained in Chapter 3. Here it is enough to emphasize that the flyfishermen who derive full satisfaction from nymph fishing are the knowledgeable ones with an interest in entomology. You can, admittedly, lure a fish by chance to take an imitation, even if it is the "wrong" fly at the moment. But this usually happens in food-poor waters where the fish do not miss any opportunity to eat.

Nutritious waters, by contrast, support fish that can afford to be fastidious. These place much stricter demands on both the right imitation and a proper presentation. The consequences are clearest during massive hatches of a particular nymph or pupa, as the fish often become very selective and will take only an exact imitation. Such occasions are normally just what distinguish the entomologically aware nymph fisherman from his wet-fly colleague.

Dry-fly
Fishing

The typical aim of fishing with dry flies is to catch the fish on the rise – those which are primarily hunting winged insects on, or near, the water surface. This is also what makes dry-fly fishing such an exciting and entertaining method. Everything that happens on the water can be followed with the naked eye.

Ideally, of course, you may first watch the fish rise, then lay out the fly, notice how it is taken, and finally make a well-timed counterstrike. But dry flies can be fished even when it is impossible to see any rising fish. With luck, they will lure a trout up to the surface and trick it into tasting them.

While the visibility of the entire process is a main attraction for many of us, we should not forget that this kind of fishing places strict requirements on our own behaviour at the water. The right imitation has to be chosen, and presented with the right equipment for trout, which are periodically shy and selective. More-over, especially with regard to smaller streams, it is naturally essential to avoid clumsy actions, either in or near the water, which can frighten the trout into "silence".

As a result, fishing with dry flies is not only a fasci-nating procedure but a literally captivating one. At the same time, it offers a true challenge and often tests the wits of whoever holds the rod.

Historical developments

A dry fly is usually defined as an imitation of a winged insect, which is fished on or in the water surface. The question of how long people have fished with such flies is then relatively easy to answer. Even if we over-look the interesting practice of using actual insects, live or dead, primitive forms of dry-fly fishing must have arisen quite long ago. For thousands of years, man has surely learned from the sight of insects that land in the water – by chance or intention – and are snapped up by fish on the rise.

Archaeologists today are fairly certain that the fish-hook, as a specific invention, appeared some 30,000 years ago. The earliest hooks, large and unwieldy to our eyes, were made of bone or wood, and eventually provided with barbs. Although the struggle for survi-val undoubtedly soon forced humans to try catching fish on hooks baited with real insects, we still know very little about this custom. Whether, and how, these "flies" succeeded in floating is another mystery which has inspired many theories.

A safe conclusion, in any case, is that throughout history our species has had good cause to turn its interest in hunting toward the waters where trout rise, and that fish which take their food at the surface have been considered a valuable source of human food.

Jig-like flies

To find informative descriptions of flyfishing – the use of a rod, line, and hooks dressed with feathers – we must wait until around 200 A.D. Claudius Aelianus, a Greek-speaking Roman author, told in his book "De Natura Animalium" that people along the Astraeus River in Macedonia hooked fish "with a spotted exterior". The flies in question do not clearly remind us of modern dry flies, but rather of jigs.

Presenting the fly upstream can be an effective variant when fishing in flowing waters. Here the dry fly is laid out obliquely upstream, to drift down toward the fish's holding places. The water must, though, have a fairly fast speed to make this technique fruitful.

Our next evidence about the sport comes from the fifteenth century, when Dame Juliana Berners published her classic article, "A Treatyse of Fysshynge Wyth an Angle" (1496). This work is important partly because it is the first testimony of fishing simply for pleasure. In addition, the writer gave a somewhat detailed account of how trout and salmon were caught with artificial flies. She also observed that the fish's diet was periodically dependent on swarming insects – the prototypes of the creations which we call dry flies. While hardly the first to notice this phenomenon, she made a pioneering contribution by putting it in print.

There are further sources in literature which mention fishing with a rod, line and hook. For example, Izaak Walton's book "The Compleat Angler" (1653), with a supplement by Charles Cotton from 1676, became a milestone in the annals of sportfishing. Already in Spain, the "Manuscrito de Astorga" (1624), written by Juan de Bergera, contained patterns and illustrations of several flies, some of which can be interpreted as dry flies according to the above definition.

Three flies from the late 1600s, shown together with their prototypes. Obviously attempts were made even then to tie flies that imitated the fish's natural food.

Refinements in dry-fly fishing

Little progress was made with this particular method during the eighteenth century. It won increasing popularity in the mid-1800s, but not at first with the use of genuine dry flies. Instead, wet flies were dried by casting them in the air, and then presented again on the water. After a short time, they began to absorb water and sank.

The dry-fly approach was introduced primarily in the southern English chalk streams, which held an abundance of both insects and hungry trout. However, only with the arrival of Frederic M. Halford did the fly patterns and their applications start to improve rapidly. His followers also developed the equipment by, for instance, making better oil-impregnated lines and more durable flies, using body materials that did not absorb water.

Halford's books, "Floating Flies and How to Dress Them" and "Dry-fly Fishing in Theory and Practice", greatly stimulated interest in the sport. Unfortunately, the "dry-fly puritans" of the day – led by Halford himself – thought that all other forms of flyfishing were immoral, and roundly condemned them. Thus, dry-fly fishing was turned into a kind of cult.

Transatlantic trends

In North America, one of the most prominent contributors was Theodore Gordon. Thanks to his correspondence with Halford, he was thoroughly familiar with English flyfishing and began to use dry flies at the end of the nineteenth century. Yet he adapted them to the local species of insects and, among other things, created the Quill Gordon which is still widely employed. A typical feature of American dry flies was that they were tied more sparsely than in Europe.

As a parallel development, dry flies for fast currents appeared. Flyfishing in England was limited to the slowly flowing chalk streams, but America offered wilder opportunities. These flies were relatively big and bushy, so that the fish could discover them easily. A later series, also popular today, were the Wulff flies, created for just such powerful running waters by Lee Wulff. Characteristics of this series – perhaps best known for the Gray Wulff – are that the wings and tail were originally tied with stag's hair, and that two hackles were wound on each side of

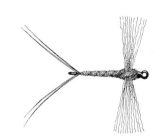

When imitating "spent spinners" – mayflies that fall dead onto the water with outstretched wings after laying eggs – the wings were once tied traditionally with feather sections. Today these are often replaced with synthetic material to make "spent polywings". On both kinds of fly, the wings and tail are divided in half by a so-called eight-tie.

Theodore Gordon, an American who – through long correspondence with Frederic M. Halford – took many hints from English flyfishing, began to fish with dry flies already in the late 1800s. After adapting the English patterns to local conditions in the USA, he created flies like Quill Gordon, which can still checkmate many a trout.

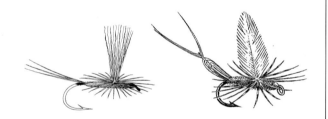

Parachute-tied dry flies have a hackle tied in horizontally – wound around the wing root. On this type of fly, too, synthetic material has become ever more common, making what is usually called a parachute-tied polywing. Such dry flies can imitate numerous species, so they are very popular on many waters.

From the mid-nineteenth century onward, it became increasingly popular to fish with dry flies – especially in the southern English chalk streams with their wealth of insects. The classic English dry flies typically have wings tied with two sections of feather quill. Such are many famous flies like Greenwell's Glory, Coachman, Blue dun and Black Gnat.

Swisher & Rickards introduced "no-hackle" dry flies, which imitate insects that are caught in the surface film and stay there while hatching. These flies, as the name shows, have no hackle but only a body, a pair of marked wings and a tail. As a result, they must be impregnated carefully in order to rest on the surface.

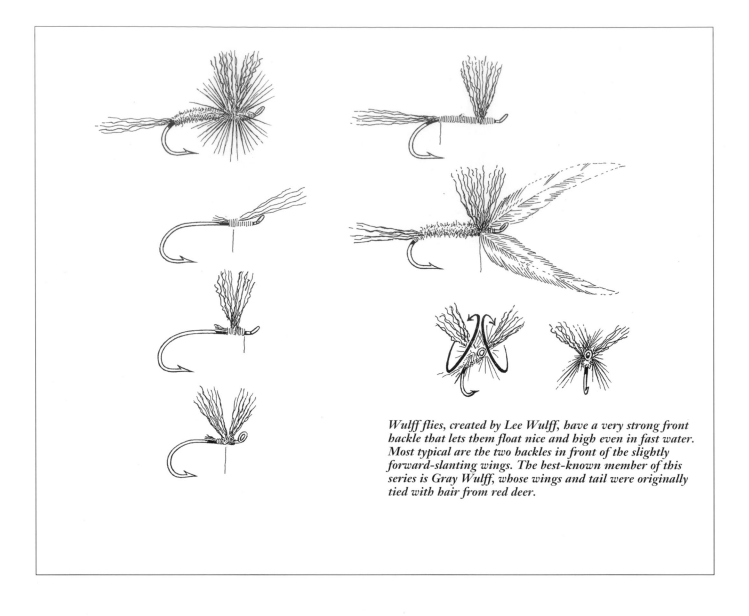

Wulff flies, created by Lee Wulff, have a very strong front hackle that lets them float nice and high even in fast water. Most typical are the two hackles in front of the slightly forward-slanting wings. The best-known member of this series is Gray Wulff, whose wings and tail were originally tied with hair from red deer.

the slightly forward-leaning wings. Consequently the flies can float amazingly well, even in the hardest currents.

The natural models

Obviously a dry fly has to imitate an insect that floats on water. The fish may also take newly hatched insects, which have struggled up to the surface in order to escape their nymph skins. But the commonest "dry" prey of trout are winged flies that are laying eggs, or have fallen half-dead, on the surface.

Mayflies and stoneflies

The insect group which has come to be most closely connected with dry-fly fishing are the mayflies. Since there are many different species of mayflies, one must decide which species to imitate for the fishing at hand. And the more selective the trout are, the more important this choice is. The species – and hence their size, body form and other characteristics – vary not only from place to place, but during the season as well. Differences also exist in body colour, wings, and tails length, between the newly hatched mayflies, or duns, and the sexually mature "spinners".

In very rapid waters, the only choice for dry-fly fishing may be a bushy Wulff fly, such as Royal Wulff (inset), presented with a stop cast.

Another insect group that is occasionally significant for dry-fly fishing are the stoneflies. These belong to the very earliest-swarming flies, often hatching soon in the spring, even before the snow has completely melted. A stonefly has two tail antennae, two antennae in front, and four wings that are laid flat along the rear body when resting. The folded wings are what, at a glance, distinguishes a stonefly from a mayfly. Since stoneflies are among the first to hatch on the water, the fish are seldom fastidious and one can often attract them up to the surface with a small stonefly imitation.

Caddis flies and terrestrials

The next large group of winged insects for the dry-fly fisherman to imitate are caddis flies. Normally grey or brown, they occur mainly in late summer or early autumn, sliding along the water surface and offering a great temptation to trout. Like stoneflies, a caddis fly has antennae on its head and four wings, but the latter are placed obliquely and resemble a house roof where they meet on the back. Perhaps the best-known caddis-fly imitation is Europea 12, but there are other effective patterns too. Not least in Scandinavia, fishing with caddis-fly imitations is very prominent, and

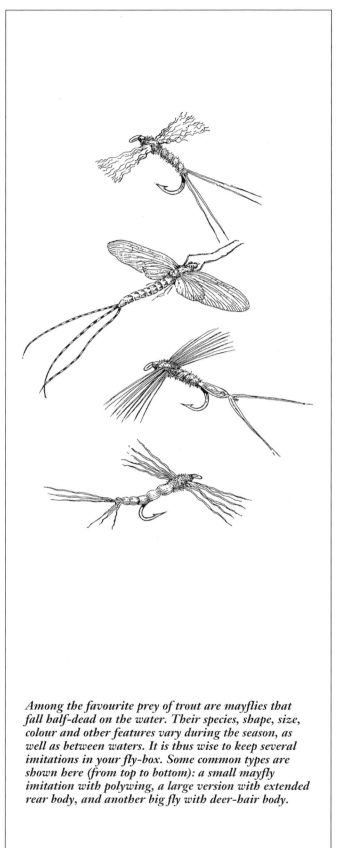

Among the favourite prey of trout are mayflies that fall half-dead on the water. Their species, shape, size, colour and other features vary during the season, as well as between waters. It is thus wise to keep several imitations in your fly-box. Some common types are shown here (from top to bottom): a small mayfly imitation with polywing, a large version with extended rear body, and another big fly with deer-hair body.

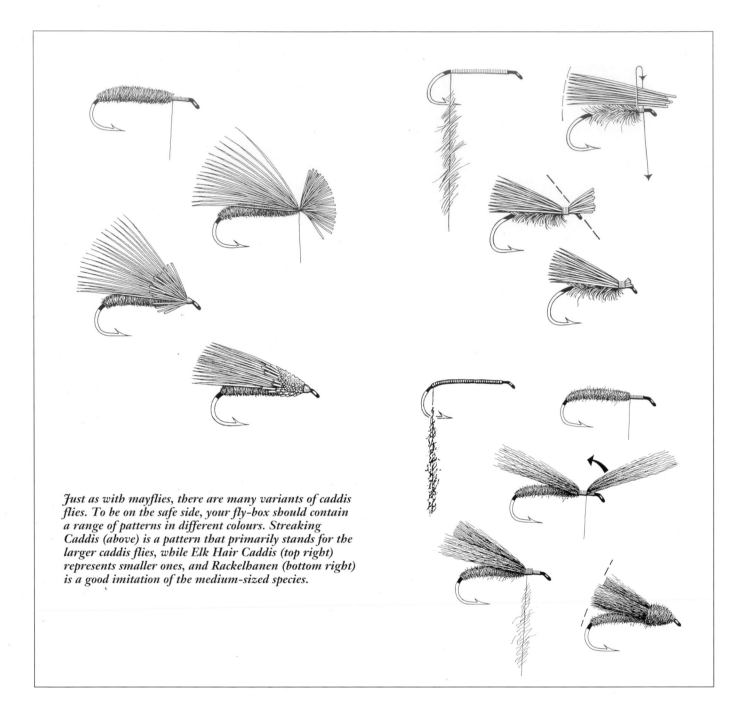

Just as with mayflies, there are many variants of caddis flies. To be on the safe side, your fly-box should contain a range of patterns in different colours. Streaking Caddis (above) is a pattern that primarily stands for the larger caddis flies, while Elk Hair Caddis (top right) represents smaller ones, and Rackelhanen (bottom right) is a good imitation of the medium-sized species.

numerous flies have been composed for this purpose, such as Rackelhanen and Streaking Caddis.

A group which should not be neglected, and whose imitations are found chiefly in the fly-boxes of inland lake fishermen, are the so-called "terrestrials" – various land bugs that happen to fall in the water and become prey for trout. In the United States, grasshoppers are doubtless the most frequently imitated. But wasps, beetles and flying ants, for example in Scandinavia, can at times stand high on the trout's menu.

The equipment

Regardless of whether dry-fly fishing for trout is done in flowing waters or still waters, a single-handed rod is used. For fishing in flowing waters, a short rod of about 8 feet is preferable, since it facilitates casting even if there are trees and bushes at the shore. But when fishing in larger waterways, a longer rod of 9 or 9.5 feet can be advantageous, in order to cast farther and guide the fly more accurately in the water. A long

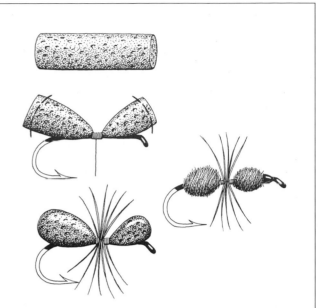

Joe's Hopper (above) is one imitation of terrestrials –
land insects – but there are simpler variants to tie, such
as the following.

Ants also dominate the trout's menu at times, when they
are swarming and tumble onto the surface – especially in
still waters. Shown at left is an easily tied imitation,
with a piece of polycelon wound on the middle of the
hook shaft. At right is an "ant" with two balls of fine-
fibred dubbing for a body.

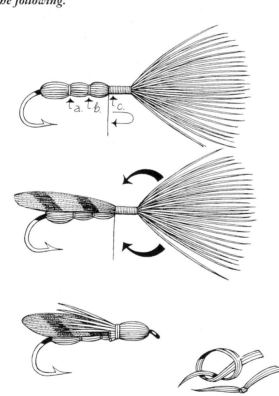

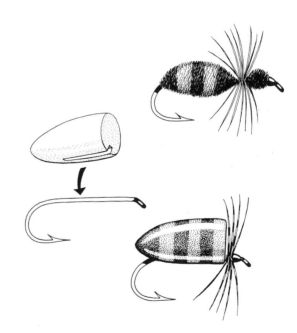

Not least for American flyfishermen, grasshoppers are
interesting because they regularly land on the water and
tempt trout. This imitation has a deer-hair body that is
attached at the bend of a streamer hook, bent forward
and tied down in sections (at a,b,c) before a new bunch is
added, bent backward and secured. The wing on its back
is made of light brown-speckled turkey.

Wasps are among the insects that occasionally land on
the surface and become trout food. Good imitations of
wasps can be made with front and rear bodies of poly
dubbing (above right), or with balsa-wood pieces that are
polished smooth and varnished in waspy colours.

rod is also helpful for fishing in still waters, where long casts may be needed in order to reach out to the fish.

As influential as the rod's length is its action. For those who choose to present their dry flies in flowing water, different casting variants may be essential, such as the roll (switch) cast – and then the rod should have a fairly slow action. On the other hand, fishing at a lake or coast often calls for long casts, making a faster and stiffer rod definitely the best choice. A further virtue of stiffer rods is that you can increase the line's speed in an air cast; thus any water absorbed by the tying material will be shaken out more quickly, and the fly's buoyancy maintained more easily. This is true even if special preparations are applied to it.

When fishing in lakes and large flowing waters, it is often a good idea to choose a long rod of 9 or 9.5 feet, which enables you to cast farther and guide the fly more easily.

The importance of taper

When selecting the AFTM class, a general rule is that one should use a lighter line and thinner leader for smaller flies, and conversely. Since dry-fly fishermen tend to work with relatively small flies, the equipment line class ought to be between 4 and 7, depending partly on whether one intends to fish in flowing or still waters.

Choosing the line is not particularly difficult in this

sport. Only a floating line, of course, can be used. But the answer is less clear when deciding between a weight-forward (WF) and a double-tapered (DT) line. Each has its advocates and opponents.

The traditional opinion is that a WF line serves better in large running waters or still-water fishing than in small streams, because it facilitates long but inexact casts. By contrast, a DT line is supposed to operate best in small running waters where an elegant presentation is more important than longer casts. In practice, however, this is of little significance.

My own experience with both types of line is that not much difference can be seen in their presentation. Normally, WF lines are tapered well enough to make the presentation fully acceptable. Nevertheless, I do think it is easier to cast with a WF line – especially

In lesser waters, however, a shorter rod is preferable. Then the fly can be presented with ease if there are trees and bushes along the shore.

when using a roll cast, for example, where one needs a certain casting weight in the few metres that hang outside the rod tip. With a WF line that is suited to the rod, you can handle a relatively wide range of situations in most waters, whether still or flowing.

It must be kept in mind, though, that the rod manufacturers' line-class markings do not always yield optimum performance. Notably the modern, rapid carbon-fibre rods can usually be loaded with a line class which is heavier than the recommended weight.

The leader's strength

Since fish that consume insects at the surface are often selective and shy, it is not advisable to use a thicker leader than necessary. But neither should you fish with such a thin leader that the fish can tear off the line too easily. It is both unsportsmanlike and foolish to attach an insufficiently strong leader.

Therefore, when choosing the leader, remember that the tip must be suited not only to the fly's size, but also to the size of the expected fish in the waters at hand. Catching a trout of 800 grams, compared to one of 5 kilograms, for instance with a hook of size 16, will place very different demands on the leader's strength.

By tradition, dry flies have been tied on hooks with an upward-bending eye. But during recent years it has become increasingly common to use hooks with a down-turned eye for these flies as well. Without going into an explanation for the former custom, one may remark that this difference does not really matter to the practical fishing. Rather, a leader with a dry fly on a down-turned hook eye will sink more easily under the water surface, and be harder for the fish to see. The inevitable result is to make the trout less suspicious.

Despite all that is written about fly patterns and how to tie them, an often-ignored detail is that the hooks must be quite sharp. You should get into the habit of whetting your hook tips before every fishing interval – not to mention when the hooks have been damaged by, for instance, striking a stone on the back cast. The fact is that even seasoned flyfishermen are frequently careless in this respect. Losing a trout because the hook is dull or, at worst, breaks off is invariably irritating. Besides, it takes at least half an hour to coax a scratched trout to rise again for the fly.

The leader's thickness must, of course, always be selected according to the conditions. But with consideration for the trout, leaders that are very thin should be avoided – it is never good to tire out a fish longer than necessary because of a weak leader.

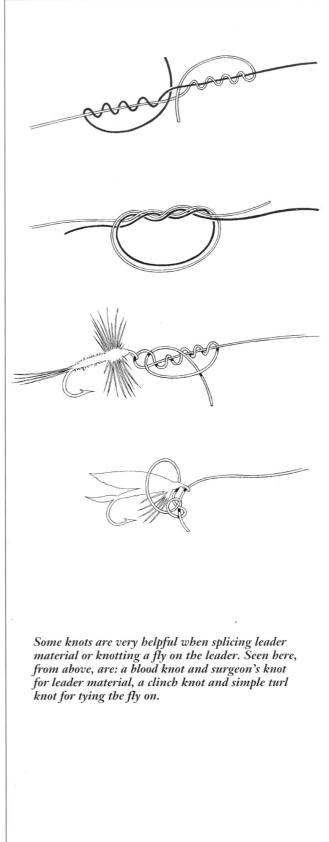

Some knots are very helpful when splicing leader material or knotting a fly on the leader. Seen here, from above, are: a blood knot and surgeon's knot for leader material, a clinch knot and simple turl knot for tying the fly on.

Practical techniques

Flyfishing in general, and dry-fly fishing in particular, require certain qualities of the sportsman: patience, quick reactions, and a good ability to observe the behaviour of fish and to draw conclusions from it. As for the last of these, it always pays off to read the water and study the insect life before starting to fish. No method can be more time-wasting and ineffective than to test the whole contents of your fly-box in search of the right fly, instead of first calmly noticing what the fish actually are eating.

In many actual fishing situations, the cast and presentation are as important as the choice of fly. The chief problem is often to make the fly drift downstream in a natural manner, and to maximize the time in which it drifts freely without dragging. Thus, you must try to exploit the currents so that the fly, leader and line maintain the same speed. Clearly, the faster the current is, and the more difficult the current conditions are, the greater will be the demands on the fisherman to present the fly while not arousing the fish's suspicion.

Exploiting the flow

The fly and line should, therefore, drift with as little hindrance as possible – and ideally with the same speed as the current – so that the fish will sense no danger. This, in turn, leaves a considerable opportunity for making different kinds of casts and their variants, which ought to be mastered if you are to fully benefit from the use of dry flies in flowing waters.

By employing the surface currents, too, good conditions can be established for the fly to drift relatively far without beginning to straggle. For example, mending the line in the proper way can prevent it from being pulled along by a fast current, which would probably force the fly to drift unnaturally. With movements of the rod and tip, it is fairly easy to make the fly drift as you like and, most importantly, where you like.

Apart from the need to take account of different current speeds, there are obstacles such as stones, which mean that the fly may not at all drift as it was intended to. A newcomer tends to regard these irregularities in the water only as problems. Yet for

A trout in flowing water, when taking an insect, rises a little downstream from its holding place, and will swim back upstream when returning to the bottom. To give it time to rise, you must therefore present the fly a little upstream from the holding place. And the deeper the fish is, the more time it needs.

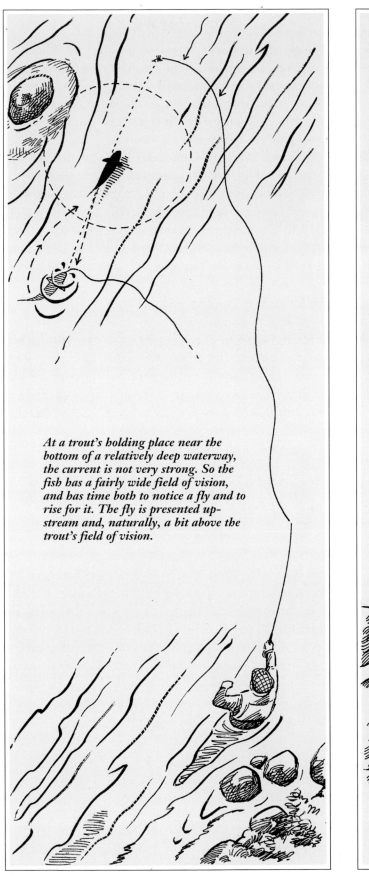

At a trout's holding place near the bottom of a relatively deep waterway, the current is not very strong. So the fish has a fairly wide field of vision, and has time both to notice a fly and to rise for it. The fly is presented upstream and, naturally, a bit above the trout's field of vision.

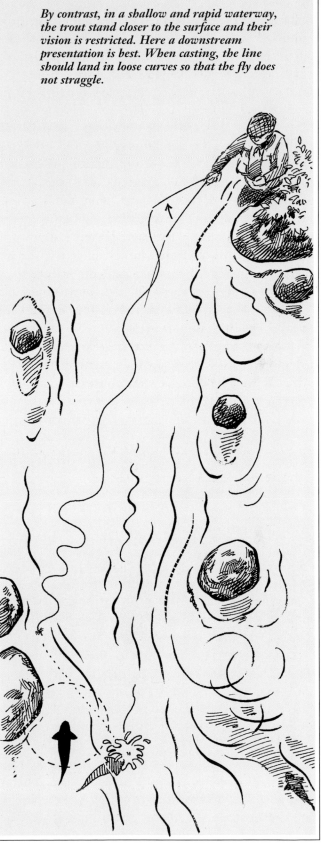

By contrast, in a shallow and rapid waterway, the trout stand closer to the surface and their vision is restricted. Here a downstream presentation is best. When casting, the line should land in loose curves so that the fly does not straggle.

experienced flyfishermen, such spots can be the ones that offer good chances of catching fish. What the fish seek are holding places to which the current transports a continuous supply of food, and which provide a current lee enabling them to eat without much effort.

Presentation in currents

When fishing in small running waters casting across and upstream is the commonest practice – and the most traditional. This is not only because the fisherman can then avoid being seen by the fish, but also because the fly can drift more freely down toward their holding place. A fly that suddenly begins to drag will certainly not win the confidence of trout. The basic objective is to make the fly imitate its natural model as closely as possible, and this refers to its behaviour on the surface as well as its appearance.

In rivers and other broad currents, however, there may be difficulties in reaching the fish by casting across or upstream, so that you have to cast in a more or less downstream direction. No matter whether you wet your flies in wide or narrow running waters, it often happens that trees, bushes and other vegetation grow right down to the shore. This, of course, may rule out the usual overhand or underhand cast. If you cannot wade out in the water, to leave space behind you for casting, the best choice is a roll cast – upstream or downstream. Since the amount of line that can be "rolled" is proportional to the rod's length, a longer rod allows the casting distance to be increased.

Variant casts

Casting techniques can be explored in greater depth, but here we need only mention some very useful types of cast. A *stop cast* is relatively simple: just before the fly hits the water, the line is pulled back with your free hand. This brakes the cast so that the leader is laid down in loose curves on the water. As the leader is not taut, the fly can drift for several metres before the leader straightens out.

Not entirely different is the *parachute cast*. When casting downstream, it is often essential in order to let the fly drift freely to the fish's holding place. The rod is stopped in the forward part of the cast, making the line stretch forward at the height of the rod tip. Then the rod tip is lowered and the fly lands on the water

with a loose leader. By lowering the tip even further, you can feed out a few more metres of line.

The *serpentine cast* is another frequent aid. By whipping the rod tip back and forth in short horizontal movements, the line is made to fall on the water in wide curves. This can be a quite effective means of preventing a fast current from sweeping the line away so that the fly is streaming.

It goes without saying that these variants become less relevant when you want a technique that allows the fly to straggle. This occurs, for example, if the fish are hunting certain insects like caddis flies, which flutter or slide across the water surface. However, such fishing is virtually impossible without high-floating and well-impregnated dry flies.

Presentation in still waters

Whereas on a running water you can cast either upstream, across or downstream, the alternatives for presenting a fly are more limited in still waters. Unless wading, or fishing from a boat or float-ring, one can only cast in a more or less wide fan-shaped sector outward from the shore edge. But even on lakes, the aim is to try and reach a known or assumed holding place – that is, either with or without rising trout – while avoiding the notice of the fish.

For dry-fly fishing on inland lakes and other still waters, the classic overhand cast has remained the most popular method, and is often most suitable as well. If the fish are not rising close to the shore, a long cast is of prime importance. In brief, you have to maximize the line's casting weight without letting the cast collapse. The length of your cast will depend largely on the line's speed. To give it an added boost, perhaps the most effective technique is that of combining the cast with one or more *double hauls*. A trained caster, using a few blind casts with a series of quick double hauls, can greatly accelerate the line and put many extra metres into the fly's trajectory.

Strategies for dry-fly fishing

Much of the dry-fly fisherman's planning must be concerned with approaching the fish in a manner that does not scare them. Not only does a fish's lateral line make it very sensitive to vibrations that are transmit-

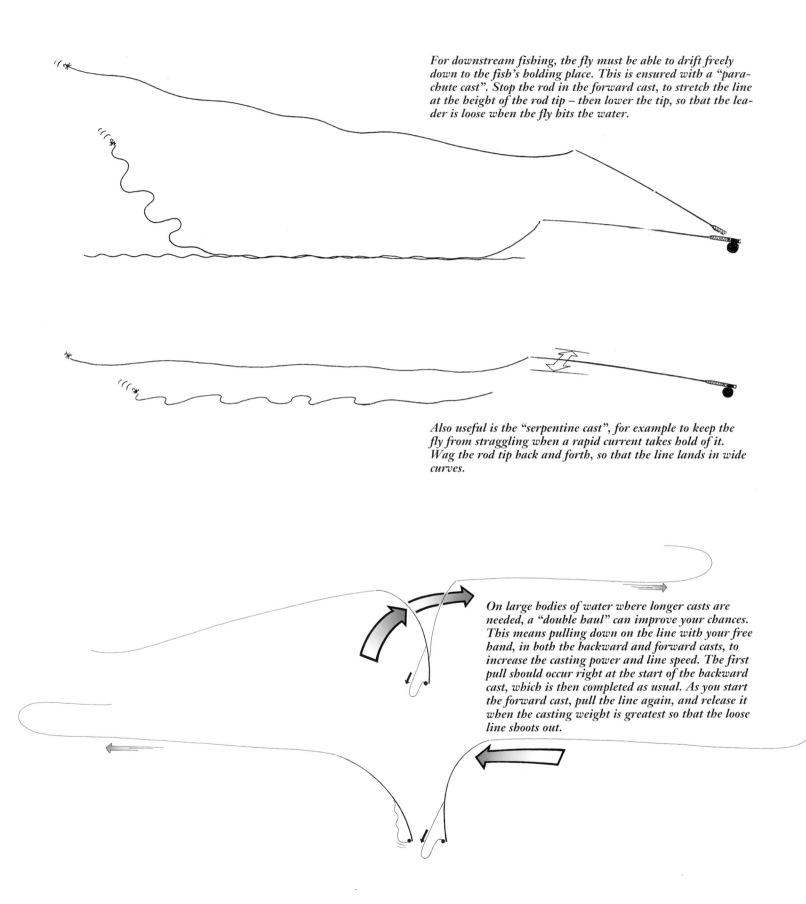

For downstream fishing, the fly must be able to drift freely down to the fish's holding place. This is ensured with a "parachute cast". Stop the rod in the forward cast, to stretch the line at the height of the rod tip – then lower the tip, so that the leader is loose when the fly hits the water.

Also useful is the "serpentine cast", for example to keep the fly from straggling when a rapid current takes hold of it. Wag the rod tip back and forth, so that the line lands in wide curves.

On large bodies of water where longer casts are needed, a "double haul" can improve your chances. This means pulling down on the line with your free hand, in both the backward and forward casts, to increase the casting power and line speed. The first pull should occur right at the start of the backward cast, which is then completed as usual. As you start the forward cast, pull the line again, and release it when the casting weight is greatest so that the loose line shoots out.

A fish can discover a fisherman easily with its sight or lateral line. You should thus try to be as inconspicuous and quiet as possible. A good approach is to use the camouflage of bushes and trees, without letting your shadow – or the fishing line's – fall on the water.

ted into the water, such as those of footsteps. It can also see up through the water surface, within its visual "window" sector. Since it has spherical eyes that move independently of each other, its field of vision is even wider than we think. Thus, one should never underestimate the fish's ability to glimpse a fisherman on land. Indeed, it may possess better means of discovering us than we have of observing it – especially in lesser running waters.

This is clearly a further reason for behaving discreetly at the shore. To approach the water as silently and carefully as an Indian is not an exaggeration. Likewise, where the water is shallow and transparent, you should seek camouflage behind, or alongside, bushes or tree trunks.

These measures, however, may not be stealthy enough. Since light rays are bent at the water surface, trout in certain positions are able to survey the surroundings as if looking through a wide-angle lens. Consequently, they may even catch sight of a fisherman who is crouching to keep as low a profile as possible. But at least it can be concluded that anyone who marches down to the water, and stands at the very edge while casting, has no real chance of catching the fish that may be lingering right at his feet.

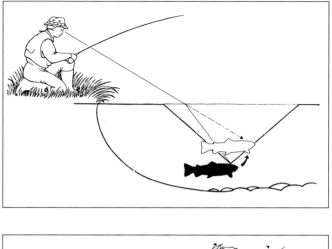

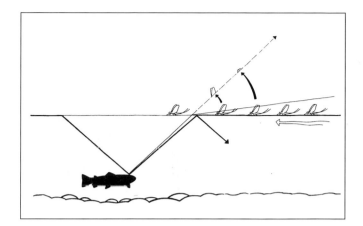

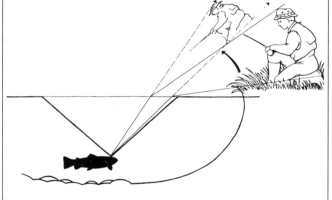

Since light rays are bent between air and water, a fish seems to stand higher than its real position at the bottom (above left).

The fish's view of the upper world is affected in the same way. A drifting insect, for instance, is noticed before entering the fish's "window". The wings are seen first, then the rest of the insect appears gradually until it is entirely within the "window" (above right).

To the fish's eyes, therefore, a fisherman is "compressed" and hovers in the air, making him visible even when he is crouching (left).

The fish's window

As a part of the fish's wide-angle perspective, its "window" has other significant implications for the dry-fly fisherman. This sector is shaped like a cone, starting at the fish's eye and spreading upward in an angle of about 97.5 degrees. The result is that, the deeper the fish's location, the more it can see above water – and the shallower it is, the less it will observe of what is going on up there.

In order to judge the distance to its prey, such as a drifting insect, the trout has to focus upon the prey with both eyes at once. And this is where the size of its "window" becomes crucial. The shallower the fish is, the more precisely you must aim your cast if the fish is to see – and perhaps take – the fly.

If the fish is standing deeper, it demands much less accurate presentation. On the other hand, it also has a longer time to watch the fly and decide whether to expect a trick or a treat. So when are your chances best? In the first case, the way in which you cast matters far more than the fly's resemblance to the natural model – while in the second case, everything may depend on the fly's size, colour and form. With good luck, the deep trout are too hungry to be choosy. But if your luck is really bad, the trout that are lingering just below the surface are the most selective ones as well.

In addition, the selectiveness of fish usually increases with the current speed. This is because the trout in a fast current simply do not have time to see what kind of food is drifting by. If they are not quick enough, the food zooms past and disappears forever.

This circumstance can be exploited by presenting the fly so that the fish have a minimum of time to study it. With such an element of surprise, one may get even a very critical trout to rise and take the fly, out of sheer fear that a piece of food will be lost. However, the surprise works best in a rapid current; when the water runs slowly, you need a more sophisticated method.

Rise rings

In contrast to fishing with wet flies, nymphs or streamers, a trout is often amazingly quick to take a dry fly. This further heightens the requirement of fast reactions on the part of the fisherman. A beginner, though, frequently makes a counterstrike so fast that the fly is torn out of the trout's mouth before it is hooked. Since the fish usually takes the fly instantly and powerfully, a calm lift of the rod tip should be enough to hook it well. The risk that the trout will spit out the fly is smaller than the chance of an exaggerated, and uncontrolled, counterstrike being ripped from its mouth. And the same is true regardless of whether you fish in flowing or still waters.

For a dry-fly fisherman, the trout's rise and the different forms of rise are, therefore, of great importance for both the choice of fly and the manner of fishing. It is no accident that the English speak of "tell-tale" rise rings. These can reveal a good deal about the kinds of insects that the fish are eating at a given time.

Forms of rise

Rises may occur with extreme caution, or enormous splashes, or anything in between. Many newcomers to the sport wrongly believe that a big fish will mean huge rise rings, and vice versa. But this is often far from the case. Large fish are careful and do not move unnecessarily, although exceptions can naturally be found.

Violently splashing rises, where you seldom see the whole fish above the water surface, indicate that the trout is taking insects which are about to fly away – for example, duns or egg-laying caddis flies, or land insects that are heading back to the shore. At the opposite extreme is a "sip rise", where the fish is standing just below the surface and can almost suck the insects into its mouth – often small bugs that are temporarily abundant on the surface.

A splash rise can be a spectacular performance. The whole fish is visible above the surface and often comes down with a flop. This sort of rise occurs when trout hunt at high speed for insects that are fluttering a little way up in the air or are about to lift off the surface.

A sip rise is formed when trout suck in, from below, insects that are on or in the surface. This is very common and creates rings of varying size. Unfortunately it can be hard to judge the fish's weight from the rings' size.

A "double-whorl rise" is rather kidney-shaped and occurs when the rising trout turns horizontally just under the surface, sweeping it into motion. But like a "swell rise", this is not a genuine rise, since the fish is taking nymphs slightly below the surface.

A "slash rise", sometimes called a false splash rise, resembles a real one but is less violent. Usually it happens when the trout turns abruptly at the surface to swim in another direction – often while hunting just under water.

A "head and tail rise" shows that the fish is taking food right under the surface. Only its back and tail fins tend to be visible, but a large trout may reveal its entire back.

A bulge rise consists of little billows formed by active trout just under water, for example when taking nymphs. The surface remains generally calm as they do not break through it.

In lakes and still parts of waterways, "cruising" fish are often seen as they methodically patrol a particular area. Rises occur at regular intervals, making it fairly easy to predict the pattern. Fishing for such trout demands anticipation and precise casts, but it's equally exciting!

In general, it is typical of fish which take insects on the water surface – namely the insects we try to imitate with artificial dry flies – that tiny air bubbles are left on the surface afterward. These bubbles appear because the fish tend to suck in a little air along with the insects.

On lakes and in calmly moving pools, especially those with rainbow trout, we commonly observe what are known as "cross-rises". A fish is often seen patrolling below the surface and regularly rising to snap up insects. Sometimes the rises occur so uniformly that you can present the fly on the fish's path well in advance, then wait for it to swim along and take.

Local variations

As with all flyfishing, the dry-fly fishing technique and strategy must be adapted to the water you are fishing in. Lakes may be either shallow or deep, and more or less nutritious or barren. A flowing water can be roaring or restful, murky or crystal-clear. The insect fauna, too, vary between different types of water, as well as with the geographical latitude.

In regard to flowing waters, the fly's buoyancy also has to suit the surface currents. A fly should float high and safely on a swift, turbulent stream. One excellent example is the bushy Wulff series created by Lee Wulff.

Thus, it is the local conditions which determine the best flies to fish with, the optimum cast to present them with, and the right technique for fishing them. While mayflies enjoy a relatively long season on the nutritious English chalk streams, caddis flies are just as predominant in, for example, Scandinavian waters. Many parts of southern North America, on the other hand, are popular places for imitations of grasshoppers – due, of course, to the fact that they catch lots of fish.

Holding places in flowing waters

Equally dependent on the type of water are the holding places of fish. In calmer, restricted flows, the trout frequently stay close to land, beneath hollowed-out shore edges or overhanging bushes, and among the protective vegetation underwater. But in larger, fast streams, they often prefer the current lee behind big stones, or below the white foam at necks and rapids.

Moreover, the alertness of fish is influenced by the kind of protection they adopt. In slow, shallow, clear waters, the trout may be very unwilling to take a fly during the daytime – whereas things can go much easier under the same conditions in a deep, fast, and perhaps murky river. As a general rule, the biggest trout have the best, and often most difficult to fish, of the available holding places. In strong currents, the

Trout choose more or less the same types of holding places in any size of waterway. Here is a section of a large waterway, where the fish may stand behind and alongside stones or plants, in front of rapid necks, in the deep water just after a rapid, in current convergences, or beneath overhanging trees.

fish commonly stand deep, making it quite difficult to attract them up to the surface. Here the greatest successes may well be reaped by wet-fly and nymph fishermen. Nevertheless, if you knot a substantial, bushy, buoyant dry fly on the leader, which even deep fish can see plainly, there is nothing but fortune to stop you from luring such monsters out of the abyss, or from winning the trout fight of your life.

Even a highly experienced flyfisherman can have difficulty in locating the trout exactly in a lake. As in waterways, though, one can "read" the water to find some likely spots. The natural conditions indicate that there are fish at stony edges and underwater banks, along vegetated shores, at deep edges, by capes and lee edges, in coves and channels, near islets and at inlets or outlets.

Presenting the flies in still waters

The characteristics of a good holding place in flowing water – from the fish's viewpoint – are that it gives the best possible camouflage and, at the same time, makes the food supply most easily accessible. On the whole, brown trout are more fastidious about the choice of a holding place than are rainbow, grayling or char. This is also valid in still waters.

While the rainbow tend to hunt actively in the free regions, the brown trout usually stand in some protected place at the bottom, often comparatively near land. For instance, they may loiter below water-lilies or fallen tree branches, from where they can make quick hunting raids to the surface and take passing insects. Frequently they stand in coves toward which the wind blows, causing a concentration of food – straight into the mouths of the trout.

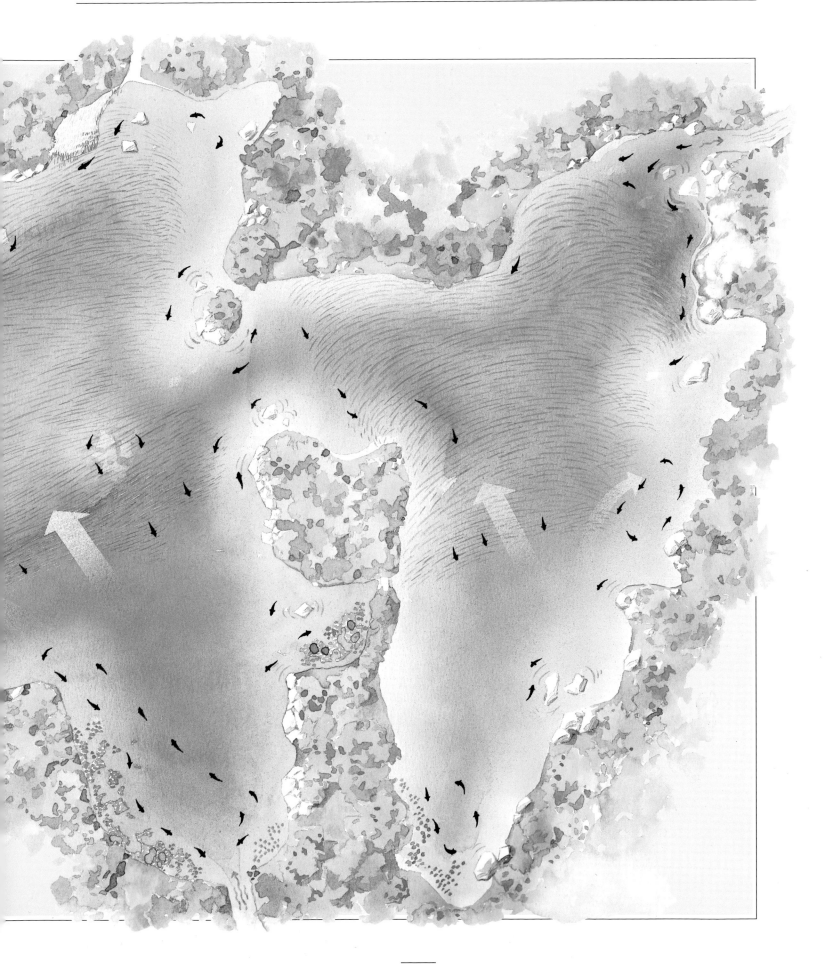

In the British Isles, a special form of boat flyfishing has developed in large lakes, with a "blowline". This somewhat thick silk line is caught up by the wind and lifts flies out onto the water. Thus one does not really cast, but simply raises and lowers the long rod to get the flies out – two or three of them. They are fished on, in, and under the surface, 5-10 metres from the boat. Besides flies, one can use a natural mayfly or even a live grasshopper, baited on a clean hook.

Similarly, fish in still water prefer to stand over shallow bottoms than near steep slopes, at least when the latter offer no protection. Other typical holding places are narrow passages between islands and peninsulas, as well as in channels and off estruarys, where the water masses are relatively mobile.

It is also in lakes that the use of boats and float-rings really becomes worthwhile. But one must keep in mind that a boat scares away the fish much more easily

Fishing with large flies

A very special variant of dry-fly fishing from a boat has been developed in the British Isles, where it is known as dapping. In its classic form, a "blow-line" is used. This is not cast in the ordinary sense, but caught up by the wind so that it carries out the fly. The boat is turned broadside to the wind, and allowed to drift over a shallow area. Thus the fly is always fished in front of the boat, so as to attract the fish before they see the floating gear.

Since inland lake trout can also be shy and selective, it is an advantage if the water surface is rippled. In sunshine and on smooth waters, the trout have far too much time to see through your tricks. A swirl on the surface from a fleeing fish may be the only sign that the fly has even been inspected.

Good advice under such conditions is to give the fly some life by pulling on the line. If you let the fly make some "noise" on the surface, it may provoke a rising fish to whirl round and attack it. This technique can also be quite effective in land-based night-fishing with relatively large dry flies.

In lake fishing, to a greater extent than when fishing in running waters, it should be remembered that trout are not only territorial, but also extremely active in the dark. Consequently – and in particular during the warm, bright summer months – the fish remain inactive near the bottom during the daytime, and wait until dusk before moving into shallow waters to take food. This is why a body of water may seem to be completely dead by day, whereas an equally patient fisherman can find his or her hands full as soon as the sun goes down...

than a belly boat. In fact, one can get quite close to the fish with a float-ring. Perhaps they mistake it for a big bird, since they sometimes rise so nearby that they can almost be caught by hand.

Regardless of whether you fish from a boat or a fbelly boat, an overhand cast is used in virtually all cases. Nor is there any good reason to complicate the outward cast, as you have plenty of room for the back-cast, and often need to make as long a cast as possible.

Fishing with Streamers and Bucktails

*M*ost of us think that fishing with long-shanked streamers and bucktails is quite a new practice – even a purely American one. But nothing could be farther from the truth. In fact, the use of these devices is probably older than any other form of flyfishing. Some even believe that the world's first description of flyfishing – by Claudius Aelianus, about 200 A.D. – had to do with authentic streamer fishing.

Such judgements can always be questioned, but it is certain that North American Indians used long-shafted "flies", tied on primitive bone hooks, beginning in the nineteenth century. We also know that Eskimos in Alaska had great success with flies whose wings were made of polar-bear hair, though they added a bone weight and a bent copper nail for a hook. These Eskimo flies were what led to the creation of the so-called "Alaska Mary Ann" fly in 1922.

American tandem flies

Real bucktails, however, go much farther back in time. One of the earliest known examples is the Fort Wayne Bucktail, red-yellow with a long white bucktail wing, used by flyfishermen in the Wild West around 1900.

But it is on the American east coast that we find the first genuine streamers, or long-shanked flies with feather wings. Here our interest focuses upon the state of Maine, which offers fine fishing for "landlocked salmon". The main action occurs in lakes, where trolling is often done with large, long-shanked flies and, commonly, tandem models having two hooks. This was the birthplace of such a classic as the Grey Ghost, a fly which has taken thousands of pugnacious lake trout since its debut in 1924. It was doubtless tied as a smelt imitation when fishing for big squaretail, but it proved to be at least as good for smelt-eating lake trout.

Effective small-fish imitations

The English, who of course brought flyfishing to North America, were no less innovative. To them goes the credit for developing monstrous double- and even treble-hooked "Demon" and "Terror" lures, notably for sea trout in brooks and rivers. Basically there was little difference between these huge English flies and the double trolling flies in Maine. They all had feather wings and were meant for really big fish.

Now we should jump to 1950, and some serious new thinking in the field. That year in America, Don Gapen tied his first "Muddler Minnow", a long-shanked fly with a clipped head and collar made of deer body hair: the air-filled hairs from the pelt, not the long tail hairs which are otherwise used for proper bucktail flies.

Don Gapen tied his Muddler Minnow as an imitation of the bottom-living "sculpins" which were an important food item for trout in his home waters. These small fish, with their wide head and body, could hardly be imitated with the flytying methods of the time. Gapen's construction was therefore creative and helpful – and his technique became the starting point for developing new ways to tie flies.

Modern streamers and bucktails

Not only flyfishing, but trout themselves, were taken by the English to New Zealand in the late nineteenth century. Down there, local flyfishermen produced a

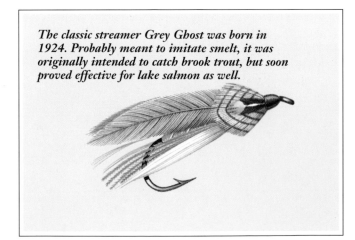

The classic streamer Grey Ghost was born in 1924. Probably meant to imitate smelt, it was originally intended to catch brook trout, but soon proved effective for lake salmon as well.

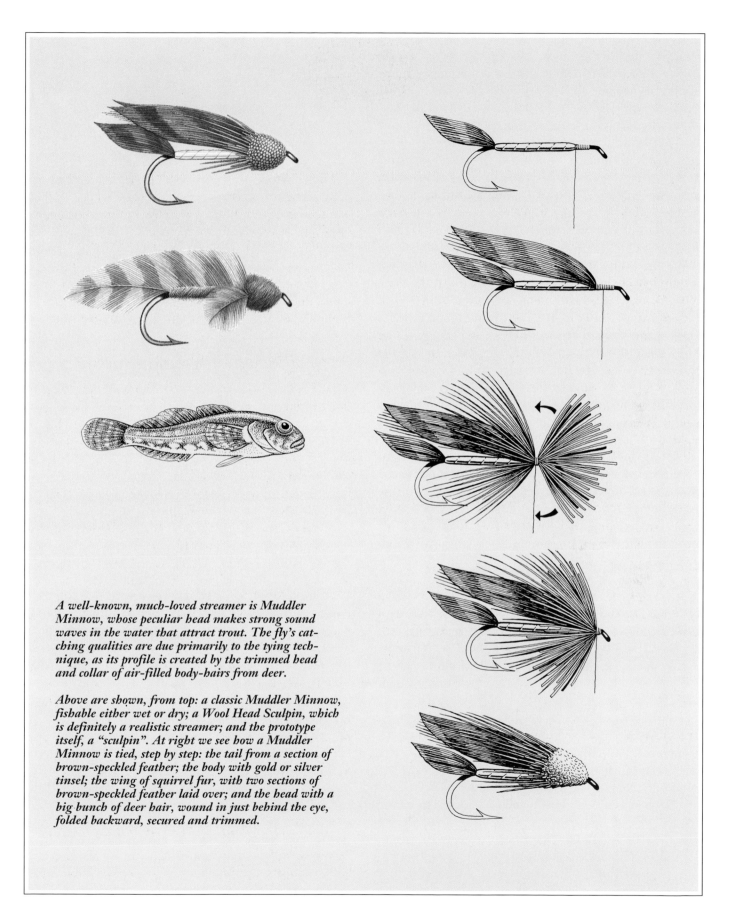

A well-known, much-loved streamer is Muddler Minnow, whose peculiar head makes strong sound waves in the water that attract trout. The fly's catching qualities are due primarily to the tying technique, as its profile is created by the trimmed head and collar of air-filled body-hairs from deer.

Above are shown, from top: a classic Muddler Minnow, fishable either wet or dry; a Wool Head Sculpin, which is definitely a realistic streamer; and the prototype itself, a "sculpin". At right we see how a Muddler Minnow is tied, step by step: the tail from a section of brown-speckled feather; the body with gold or silver tinsel; the wing of squirrel fur, with two sections of brown-speckled feather laid over; and the head with a big bunch of deer hair, wound in just behind the eye, folded backward, secured and trimmed.

rather odd type of fly, which can also be called a kind of streamer: the now-famous Matuka. What is special about a Matuka is the wing. Instead of fluttering free as on normal streamers, it is tied over the body and, consequently, cannot easily wind itself around the hook bend.

The Matuka has gone out of fashion these days, but the idea behind it has survived in modern "zonker" flies, where the feather wing is exchanged for a thin strip of rabbit fur. This method of tying gives solid flies with a marked profile – though, unfortunately, flies that absorb a lot of water and become heavy to cast with. Zonkers are provided with a body of braided mylar, which makes very realistic small-fish imitations.

But the most true-to-life streamer flies must be "wool-head sculpins". These take after the very same bottom-living small fish that inspired the Muddler Minnow. Their origin lies in the fact that flies with a classic head and collar in the latter style do not sink well, being made with air-filled hairs. And since sculpins live not only at, but virtually on, the bottoms of many flowing waters, the Muddler Minnow is actually not ideal for its purpose.

The "wool-head sculpin" definitely is, because it replaces the muddler head with a water-absorbent head of clipped wool. In addition, it has breast feathers from – for instance – partridge, which superbly imitates the broad breast fins that sculpins are equipped with. the rest of the fly is often tied in traditional Matuka fashion with a feather wing, tied down over the back.

On a Matuka streamer, the wing feathers are wound tight along the whole body. But before they are laid on the hook shaft, the fibres on the two hackle feathers' undersides must be torn loose. When attaching the feathers to the head, you wind the ribbing carefully forward through the wing, fasten it at the head, and tie in a false hackle.

Zonkers are a development of Matuka streamers, simply replacing the feather wing with a thin strip of rabbit-skin to mark the profile better. The body is of braided mylar tube, which further strengthens the fly's resemblance to small fish.

Fantasy flies versus imitations

In general, we distinguish between featherwinged streamers and the hairwinged bucktail flies. Today, however, these are made of other hair materials than bucktail. As a rule, whereas streamers with simple feather wings are most effective when the current is not too hard, a strong current calls for bucktails with stiffer hair wings that do not "collapse" in the flow. There is also a distinction between flies based on pure fantasy and the ones that resemble small fish in a convincing manner. The classic Grey Ghost was, and is, a smelt imitation – even if we would consider it a bad imitation today. Conversely, we now have very good small-fish imitations like the Black Nosed Dace, and the trio of flies that copy trout fry – the Little Brown Trout, Little Rainbow Trout and Little Brook Trout. This trio, admittedly, shows that all trout are cannibals, glad to feast on their own species whenever they get the chance!

Synthetic materials

Flies are traditionally tied with hair and feathers when it comes to natural materials. But synthetic components are playing an important role in ever more flies. The most explicit representative of modern artificial flies is certainly the Danish Juletrae ("Christmas Tree"), which consists essentially of mylar in diverse colors. The original form, with its mother-of-pearl hue, is an excellent imitation of smelt and other small fish. In more garish versions, fluorescent or even phosphorescent, it becomes a pure fantasy but still catches very well. Not least the orange-red variety is a high scorer on both trout and salmon all over the world – perhaps because it reminds them of a red shrimp.

A classic bucktail like the red-yellow Mickey Finn has usually been regarded as a pure fantasy fly – an "attractor" that can lure fish with its exaggerated colours. But we should keep in mind that many small fish, even silvery ones, shine with all the colours of the

(Right) Thunder Creek, an American type of fly, is another very good imitation of small fish. Depending on what kind of small fish are in the water at hand, the fly is adapted in colour and size to match the trout's food. Begin by tying in a thin, backward-pointing wing of bucktail on the hook shaft. Then tie in a bunch of dark hair on top, and a light bunch – pointing forward – below. Fold them back and fasten with the tying thread.

Polystickle is a simple and effective imitation of, for example, a small minnow or a stickleback. This pattern, most popular among lake and coastal flyfishermen, can be varied at will by changing colours on the body (of floss and/or polythene), back and tail (of raffene), and hackle.

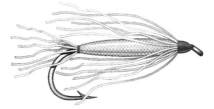

The Danish fly Juletrae is an excellent representative of those that are built up with synthetic plastic materials. This modern "synthetic fly" consists almost entirely of braided mylar tubing, whose colours and nuances are highly variable.

rainbow when the sun is on them. Colourful flies such as Mickey Finn may therefore easily resemble little fish, at least to a fish's eye.

Otherwise, it can be concluded that food-seeking fish are best offered good imitations of their natural prey, and that dazzling fantasy flies are most appropriate for provoking fish to strike. This is especially true of aggressive salmon and trout when spawning. Here it can be advantageous to use flies of the same spawning colours, which suggest possible competition. Male fish are particularly apt to fall for this trick!

Equipment for streamer fishing

When you fish with streamers and bucktails, the flies on your leader tend to be big – and so do the fish you are after. As a result, the gear for such fishing has to be

a bit stronger than normal, so that you can cast such flies and can handle large fish in hard currents.

For fishing in minor streams and lakes, where the fish are seldom big and the flies do not need to be either, you can get along fine with a 9-foot fly rod of class 5-6, a fly line and a long leader with a 0.20-mm tip.

But if you want to use a single outfit for all streamer and bucktail fishing, it should be a rod of 9-10 feet in class 7-8. According to the conditions of water current and depth, a floating or sinking line will be on the reel, which must also be able to hold 100 metres of backline.

In flowing waters with many large stones, a sink-tip line is well worth having. The sinking tip reaches down to the fish while the floating main line can be mended to avoid snagging on stones. The leader, 0.25-0.30 mm, should be fairly short when fishing with a fast-sinking line. Here a long leader would only hold the fly up, away from the fish.

Tackle for heavy fish

The above equipment is enough for most streamer fishing in rivers, lakes and the sea. However, in the cases mentioned last, it may be very rewarding to use an intermediate line instead of the traditional floating line – particularly when there are waves on the water. A floating line tends to follow the billows, thus weakening the contact out to the fly. But an intermediate line sinks under the waves, ensuring a taut line to the streamer or bucktail. And this difference can certainly be noticed in the number of hooked fish.

In large rivers with hard currents, and when fishing in the sea over steep slopes in deep water, there may be a need for even stronger gear. A good choice is a stiff 9-foot rod in class 9-10, with a fast-sinking WF line or – to get far down – shooting heads that sink at different speeds. The heavy shooting line enables the head to sink freely and as rapidly as possible. Use a leader of 0.30-0.40 mm.

Generally the leader's length should be 12 feet for a floating line, 9 feet for an intermediate line, 6 feet for a sink-tip, and 3 feet for the fastest sinking lines. This will give optimal fishing with long-shanked flies.

Why streamers and bucktails?

There are plenty of ways to flyfish for trout, each having its own benefits and drawbacks. Downstream wet-fly fishing is the beginner's favourite, as the current solves any problems in presentation and, at the same time, maintains a taut line out to the fly. Dry-fly fishing is, for many of us, the most fascinating method of all, since it allows the fish to be seen rising to a correctly placed fly. However, in terms of annual catch, there can be no doubt that the most fish are taken, right over the bottom, by proper fishing with weighted nymphs.

This brings us back to fishing with long-shanked streamers and bucktails – a method which, unfortunately, is overlooked by many flyfishermen. Not only

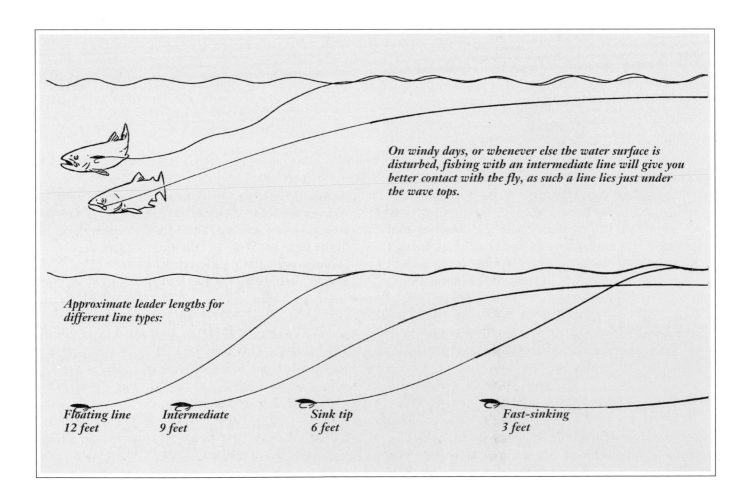

On windy days, or whenever else the water surface is disturbed, fishing with an intermediate line will give you better contact with the fly, as such a line lies just under the wave tops.

Approximate leader lengths for different line types:

*Floating line
12 feet*

*Intermediate
9 feet*

*Sink tip
6 feet*

*Fast-sinking
3 feet*

is it wonderfully simple, but it almost invariably yields the biggest fish!

How can these advantages go together? As long as a trout is small, it feeds mainly on insects and crustaceans. But as it grows, it becomes ever more interested in larger prey – namely small fish. Big trout rarely eat tiny insects or crustaceans, which are just what a flyfisherman normally imitates with his nymphs and dry flies. Instead, big trout want a mouthful that contributes most to their growth. Obviously, then, a flyfisherman who sticks to streamers and bucktails will eventually walk off with the biggest trout in the water.

So it is no coincidence that Americans – who have virtually invented this kind of fishing – speak of streamers and bucktails as "big fish flies". Large fish are looking for ample meals, and these are what substantial flies provide.

Simple methods

Fishing with long-shanked flies is straightforward by comparison with using dry flies and nymphs. The latter involve practical problems which never arise in strea-

Bucktails and streamers are usually on the leader when we fish for big trout. Suitable for this fishing, therefore, is a fairly robust rod of 9-10 feet in AFTM class 7-8, ideally with a short butt.

mer fishing. In the first place, you have to estimate the current when presenting a dry fly or nymph to the fish in a realistic manner. The current keeps overtaking such small flies and makes them drag, moving more slowly than the water. Once a fish sees this, it knows that the fly is not food and should be avoided!

Things are rather different when you have a big streamer or bucktail on the leader. These, of course, are flies that imitate small fish. And small fish are strong swimmers which – to a much greater extent than tiny insects or crustaceans – can defy the current and even swim against it, at least for short distances. Small fish also swim fairly fast if they need to. As a result, you can hardly fish a streamer or bucktail wrong in relation to the current. Certainly some methods are more effective than others in getting fish to strike. But the presentation is usually by no means as critical with a large, long-shanked fly as with a little nymph or dry fly.

Finally, there is a special obstacle for nymph fishermen. Often the nymph goes so far down, or the water is so murky, that the fish itself cannot be seen. Since the fish strikes cautiously, opening its mouth and sucking the nymph in, it may be extremely difficult to discover before it notices its mistake and spits out the fly. So a nymph fisherman must be clever and rely on strike indicators in order to register strikes at all.

Many advantages

Such problems are not confronted with a streamer or bucktail. What you then experience are hard, constant strikes, and the fish often hook themselves solidly. Your line is always taut out to the fly, and you take it in with much larger sweeps, as well as at higher speeds, than a nymph fisherman does. The consequence is that you can normally leave the hooking to the fish – as long as your hook is sharp, which it should be! With hooks of this size, correct sharpening is particularly important.

On the whole, fishing with streamers and bucktails has so many advantages that one wonders why it does not enjoy the same popularity as dry-fly and nymph fishing. Some people call it a trivial or primitive method, but the opposite holds. It can be just as refined as the fisherman makes it. The opportunities for variation are infinite!

In spring and autumn, using big long-shanked flies is often the only possible way of coming into contact with the fish. During these seasons the water is commonly high, cold and murky: conditions in which the fish stay on the bottom, and only when necessary do they move far to catch a fly. A large streamer or bucktail, glittering in sunlight and sparkling with colours, on a fast-sinking line with a short leader, is then a recipe for success – and there may well be no other. If the fly is to be visible, it must be big and be placed right under the fish's nose in the dark water.

Provocation fishing

A quite different application is fishing for aggressive fish in their spawning season. All trout species are more or less aggressive when approaching this period. As they acquire mating colours and – in the males – a frightening hook on their lower jaw, they become increasingly pugnacious and territorial. Moreover, they have often stopped hunting for food. The fly-fisherman can exploit these traits by presenting large flies which intrude on the fish's territory, not least on that of the males.

In this special kind of fishing, patience and local knowledge are essential to the outcome. The fish has to be located exactly, so that the fly can be presented right in front of it – and frequently several times before it is persuaded to strike. Your compensation is enormous excitement and, not seldom, the biggest fish of the year. However, these are discoloured spawning fish, of scant value on the dinner-table, and should be released with thanks for the fight. They are worth a good deal more in the spawning waters than at home in your kitchen!

Techniques in flowing waters

Streamers and bucktails can be fished by many specific methods, but fortunately there are a few fundamental ones that apply to diverse conditions. Before making your choice, you must know where the fishing is to take place. Will it be in flowing or still waters? And in the latter case, will you fish from land or from a boat?

When fishing for aggressive, spawning trout, large provocation flies are used, and presented so that they violate the fish's territory to irritate it. Typically, such fish stretch out their fins and bend their backs up.

Further, a boat fisherman has to decide whether his vessel will stay anchored or drift with the current.

Once all this is clear, the methods are well-defined and easy to adopt. A lot of flyfishermen, though, have little insight into the technical background of these methods, and therefore do not get as much out of them as is possible. It definitely pays off to learn the techniques thoroughly before you start fishing.

When talking about currents in relation to fishing methods, there are basically two directions: upstream and downstream. This may sound banal, but it underlies a proper grasp of the methods used.

Fishing downstream

Traditional wet-fly fishing is done downstream. You cast the fly at some angle across the current, as well as downstream. Then the current takes the line and swings it alongside your bank of the water. This method is equally good for river and sea trout, generally with

When a trout takes a bucktail or streamer, the strike is often quick and hard. Usually the fish hooks itself – perhaps because we tend to fish with a taut line and take in the fly rather fast with long pulls.

wet flies and large streamers. It is also how most people use their long-shanked flies, often without the slightest imagination: in other words, mechanical fishing.

The line may be either floating, sinking, or sink-tip. If the water is low and clear, a floating line and a long leader are excellent with small flies. But if it is high and cold, you can do better with a sinking line – preferably a WF, which is weighted in front, towards the fly. Combined with a short leader, this should bring the fly down to the fish.

In a troublesome current, with many obstacles that create turbulence, it is necessary to "mend" the line regularly, so that the fly keeps moving correctly in the

water. For this purpose a floating line is ideal, but it will not go down deep. A sinking line will, but cannot be mended. In such situations the right choice is a sink-tip line. The fly descends on its drooping end, while its floating main line is easy to mend if the fly strays.

When the current is slow, your casting has to favour the upstream direction. This gives the current more time to pull the line and make the fly move faster. But in a rapid current, you should cast far downstream, as straight as possible. Otherwise the fly will have too little time to swing in, and its speed through the water becomes much too great.

If you use a sinking line, be prepared to release extra line into the current, after the line and fly are cast out. Thus the line will have time to sink, before the current takes it and swings the fly across – as well as upward in the water. In really deep water, you may need to let out several metres of extra line, which is most feasible with a WF line.

Once the fly starts swinging across the current, it may begin to drag on the surface. This can be counteracted – unless the current is too strong – by simply lowering your rod tip, thus decreasing pressure

Fishing in a strong current frequently calls for flies tied with stiffer materials. One must also adapt one's fishing to the fact that the current carries the line away rapidly and, thus, the fly covers the water at high speed. This can be compensated by continually mending the line.

on the line. If that is not enough, and the fly goes on streaming, you can mend the line upstream as mentioned already.

Activating the fly

By contrast, in very slow water such as deep hollows and pools, the fly may sink quite lifelessly through the weak current. A fly like this cannot catch fish, so you have to revitalize it. Lift the rod tip and, if necessary, take in slack line with your left hand. Large, calm pools should be regarded as still water with no current, and call for the same technique as in lakes and the sea: the fisherman himself must give life to the fly in the water.

As the fly swings across the current, you follow it slowly with your rod tip pointing towards it. Occasional jerks of the rod tip will enliven the fly – or else it can be allowed to swing freely. Which procedure is most effective remains a matter of debate: each has champions and critics, but none of them is right all the time!

Eventually the fly reaches your own bank, and you can either take the line in for a new cast, or – if the water is deep and may contain holding places – leave the fly a while to dangle them. Often an indecisive trout will have come in close to the bank, where it lingers and watches the fly. If it sees no more movement, it will swim out again. Taking in line rapidly with your left hand is then a good way of getting the fish to strike.

What we have just described is the traditional "cross-stream and downstream" method of fishing flies. It works as well with small wet flies as with big streamers. But small flies drag much more easily – losing their credibility, from the viewpoint of the fish – than do large streamers and bucktails. The latter can be fished boldly in all directions relative to the current, without seeming unnatural to the fish.

But a slow current offers very different conditions. Besides needing flies of softer material, you should, for example, cast more upstream – since you now want the current to take the line and give the fly more speed. Here, too, of course, the speed can be controlled by mending the line.

Mature fish

A variant of this classic method can be used for sluggish fish that are ready to spawn. These may have long since ceased to hunt, and must be irritated or provoked to strike. Here is a challenging sport which, as noted previously, requires local knowledge and plenty of patience. At the opposite extreme are, for example, trout that eat actively and tend to strike as soon as they see the fly. The same is often true of fresh-run sea trout, steelhead and Arctic char, when they have been in fresh water for only a short time and still retain their marine striking reflex. Under those conditions, you can quickly fish large areas of a waterway while moving downstream at a good pace.

Heavy spawning fish are far less responsive. They

165

seldom react when they first see the fly pass. So if you fish the water at the same tempo as you did earlier in the season, you will seldom catch anything. Instead, gear down and concentrate your effort on a few chosen holding places – or even better, on individual fish.

Coaxing the fish to take

If you know where a holding place is, or can actually see it, position yourself upstream of the fish, as directly as possible. The distance should not be too great: 10-15 metres is enough. Then cast your big, colourful, provocative fly down towards the fish. If there is no reaction, let the fly swing back and forth in the current before the fish. It will become ever more disturbed about the intruder's impudent behaviour. A clear view of the fish will reveal that it twitches its fins at the rate of its rising temper!

Often the fish's initial response is to rush forward and attack the fly – without being hooked. Probably it will not even take the fly in its mouth, but only deliver a blow. But when it finds that the fly does not go away, and that tougher action is needed to remove the thing from its territory, it will strike hard and, as a rule, hook itself firmly enough to be landed.

Night fishing

Another special variant of the classic downstream method is night fishing. As we know, large trout of the species *Salmo trutta* are among the most active fish at night. By day, we rarely catch sight of them, since they stay hidden in deep hollows or in the shadows of fallen trees and overhanging banks. They are also big fish that have stopped eating insects or crustaceans in favour of small fish – commonly their own offspring. Hence they are perfect targets for the streamer fisherman who is willing to sacrifice his sleep.

The technique in this case is, once again, cross-stream and downstream; yet the flies are unusual. Night flyfishing has its own theoretical background, with which the fish agree entirely. At night they can best see their prey in the upward direction, because the sky – despite its darkness – is always brighter than other surroundings. Consequently, most night flyfishing is done with a floating line and large streamers or bucktails. These not only have a prominent silhouette against the sky, but also create pressure waves in the water that can be sensed by the fish.

Flies with a Muddler-like collar and head are therefore ideal for night fishing. So are big zonkers with ample wings made of rabbit fur. Such flies must be considerably larger than those used in daytime – by at least two hook sizes. Normally the flies are welcome to "bulge" in the surface water without breaking through it. Flies that straggle right in the surface layer are excellent. No rules exist for whether one of these kinds is better than the other, but it is worthwhile to experiment.

Fishing upstream

Fishing upstream with streamers and bucktails is seldom done. Nearly all streamer fishing employs the cross-stream and downstream technique. However, in some situations an upstream presentation is both the only, and the best, means of getting a strike.

For a flyfisherman, this method is much more laborious than the traditional one. Repeated casts are necessary, and the current keeps bringing the fly back. Neither does the method permit you to fish long stretches of water efficiently. Sending streamers and bucktails upstream should, instead, be treated as a supplementary technique – for places where a downstream presentation either is impossible or has yielded no results.

The upstream procedure is especially effective when you want to fish a deep current below your own or the opposite bank. Trout often hold and hide there – in the daytime usually well beneath the overhang, which makes them feel secure. They can be incredibly difficult to reach with a downstream presentation, as the current immediately pulls the fly away from the productive water.

Dead drift

The solution is to lay a long cast upstream, then take in line at a fast rate, so that the fly moves more quickly than the current. Your line should literally race in, if the method is to be effective. On the other hand, you can count on getting strikes so powerful that you almost lose your grip on the rod!

Trout are nocturnally active fish. As a result, an area of water that holds only small trout in the daytime can yield surprisingly big ones at night – taken, for instance, on a streamer fished near the surface and across the current.

In the white-foaming water under rapids and falls, it can pay to fish a large streamer upstream. But this "dead drift" method requires a fast counterstrike, as the fish tend to take a freely drifting streamer calmly and carefully.

Occasionally it is enjoyable to fish a large streamer upstream by "dead drift", like a big nymph. This pays off primarily in the white-foaming water beneath waterfalls. The trout here are accustomed to seeing small fish thrown down to them, more or less stunned, by the strong current. They find these small fish easy prey, and are thus also glad to eat a freely drifting streamer – ideally a weighted "wool-head sculpin". But you should not expect any violent strikes: a trout will just lap up the fly as if it were nibbling a helpless nymph, not feeding greedily. Such fish cannot be hooked without dealing a rapid counterstrike.

Techniques in still waters

The currents in lakes and the sea are rarely sufficient to be fought against. Neither are they enough to give a fly life. The flyfisherman must therefore do so, by taking in line with his left hand. Indeed, the water moves too slowly to keep the line stretched and make the fish hook itself when it strikes. You have to be watchful all the time, ready to punch back at the slightest jerk of the line.

Naturally, this rule has exceptions. When fishing with a floating line, a brisk crosswind can have the same effect on the line as a current in a waterway, though the fly hangs down in the motionless water. You then have all the advantages of a taut line – as long as the wind is not too hard. A crosswind should be exploited to the utmost, if you are fishing along a coast with the wind at your back. It will not only hold the line taut, but also lengthen your cast. To fish in the opposite direction with streamers and bucktails is both tiresome and foolish!

Streamer fishing in the sea

The sea often brings tidal currents, which enable your line, leader and fly to behave much as they do in a waterway. These currents can, of course, be harvested with the same methods as in rivers – by casting across the current or fishing gradually downstream. You can thus cover a large area in a relatively short time. The only problem arises when the wind and current are going in opposite directions, and with modest force. Your luck will be hopeless if you use a floating line that might drift in either direction. The answer is to substitute an intermediate line, as it can sink beneath the wind-blown surface.

If there are low waves with no current, it can be difficult to maintain contact out to a streamer or bucktail. Once more, you have to give up the floating line and use an intermediate type. While the former tries to follow the waves, the latter descends through them and allows you to keep a straight line to the fly.

Taking in the fly

When taking in the fly, several factors come into play: the size of the fly, and the temperature and depth of the water. To begin with, a rather simple relationship exists between the fly's size and the speed it should be

fished with. Small streamers do not behave very con-vincingly if they are fished at a tempo which no small fish could imitate. By contrast, large bucktails can be fished rapidly, and often with amazing success. A big fly, brought home at a breathless rate, will frequently get a strike from a fish which, otherwise, would only follow it back with interest – right to the tip of the rod.

Secondly, the water temperature is decisive for the fly's speed through the water. In winter, when the water is cold, the fish are correspondingly sluggish, so there is no point in fishing a fly fast and high. It should travel slow and deep, at the level of such fish and at a tempo they can follow. Slow fishing is also a necessity if the fish stand deep – as well as if the water happens to be warm. A fast fly will rise immediately to the surface, away from the fish.

Clear choices

The fly can be kept down by using a sinking line, but this is avoided by many coastal fishermen. A sinking line is much harder to control than a floating line

In lakes, along coasts and in other extensive waters, you should exploit the wind as much as possible, for example by always trying to fish with your back to it. Thus your casts will be lengthened and the line kept taut – a way of fishing that has proved its value here.

when you are fishing from land. On the other hand, boat fishermen have no problems with sinking lines and can use them wherever the conditions are suitable.

Although these comments about taking in the fly may seem obvious, they are seriously violated in prac-tice by quite a few fishermen, who consequently fail to catch what they are after!

Streamer fishing from land, in either lakes or the sea, is almost always done with a floating line or inter-mediate line. The above methods are employed as regards both covering the water and taking in the fly. If you fish while wading, the cast should be laid right in front of you, with the wind at your back if possible. Headlands, rocky islets and the like can be fished by flicking your casts from a fixed position. Over slopes or belts of vegetation, it is preferable to cast along them rather than across them, as the fly then has more time to fish effectively.

Boat fishing

Fishing from a boat is somewhat more complicated. A boat certainly provides access to places and depths that lie out of reach for the shore fisherman. Likewise, it enables the fisherman to sneak up on the fish.

In other words, there are many advantages with a boat – but at the same time it demands much more of the user. A flyfisherman who works from a boat must not only have good insight into the technique. Proper handling of the craft is essential for successful fishing; otherwise it is often a hindrance rather than a help.

First comes the difference between fishing from a drifting boat and from an anchored boat. If you decide to use the boat simply as a means of extending your casts, then you have to position it so that you can cast over places which you think are productive, anchoring it within reach of the fish. This approach is best applied to localities where the bottom plunges down over cliffs. Just at the transition from shallow to deep waters, trout are apt to linger. So you anchor the boat inside the cliff, pointing out toward the depths. The line should be a sinking WF – a shooting head, to get

very far down – which is cast over the deep water and allowed to sink freely. The fly is taken in by the same method described earlier, with a clear emphasis on relatively heavy equipment and large flies.

From a drifting boat

If you choose to anchor the boat, look for a well-defined and limited fishing spot: typically one where the fish come by frequently as they hunt smaller fish. From this vantage, you cannot fish out any considerable area with streamers and bucktails. But you can do so from a drifting boat, which keeps moving with the wind and current – assuming that you are not totally becalmed, as seldom happens. In small lakes, a boat sometimes scarcely moves at all, and you fish the same amount of water as from an anchored boat. But in large lakes, and especially at sea, there is always a current even on windless days; so you can be virtually certain of being able to fish from a drifting boat, and cover sizable areas with your streamers and bucktails.

Thus, if you want to fish from a freely drifting boat, there should be some wind or current to move it while you are fishing. However, the wind may become too strong and push the boat so fast that you cannot fish effectively. Luckily a solution is available: you cast a drogue overboard. It operates like a parachute brake against the boat's drift across the water.

Where and how the fly should be taken in depends, among other things, on the water's depth and temperature, as well as the fly's size. Small flies should be recovered slowly, while big ones can move faster without losing their credibility. When the water is cold and the fish sluggish, the fly must be fished at the bottom, whereas in warmer water it can be taken in quickly and thus shallowly.

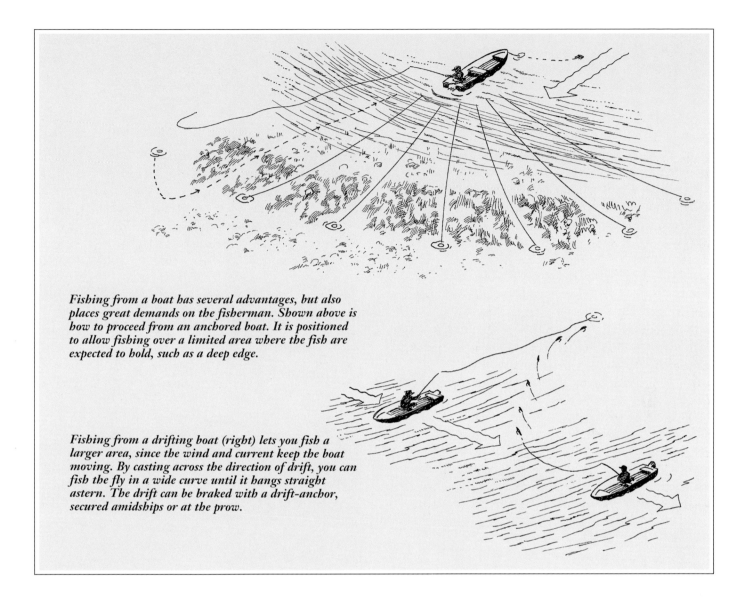

Fishing from a boat has several advantages, but also places great demands on the fisherman. Shown above is how to proceed from an anchored boat. It is positioned to allow fishing over a limited area where the fish are expected to hold, such as a deep edge.

Fishing from a drifting boat (right) lets you fish a larger area, since the wind and current keep the boat moving. By casting across the direction of drift, you can fish the fly in a wide curve until it hangs straight astern. The drift can be braked with a drift-anchor, secured amidships or at the prow.

Normally a drogue is fastened amidships, since the boat tends to drift sideways. But if the wind is very hard, it can be worth attaching the drift anchor at the stem instead. As a result, the boat will drift pointing into the wind. This creates less wind resistance and further decreases the speed of drift.

Casting in the direction of drift

Traditional boat fishing – as practised in the British Isles – is done with a team of small wet flies, which are cast at short distances in the direction of the boat's drift. Often they are barely reel-cast. Once the flies are on the water, the rod tip is raised gradually as the boat drifts, and line is eventually taken in. The aim under all conditions is that the flies should fish rather slowly through the water – like small nymphs and pupas, heading for the surface in order to hatch. Farthest up on the leader, there is usually a bob-fly, a densely hackled Palmer fly, whose job is to straggle in the surface water.

Long-shanked streamers and bucktail flies, though, are not fished in this manner. They are supposed to imitate small fish, which swim a lot faster. Here it is much better to cast out across the boat's drift direction – preferably with long casts, if the weather is calm and the waves are insignificant. While the boat moves with the wind and current, the flies will tend to swing in a wide bow, until they are hanging right behind the boat. Then you can retrieve them for a new cast, once more across the drift direction.

This is quite an efficient method, and covers a large

water area in a short time. Naturally, it is easiest if you fish with a floating line. Yet the latter is not always sufficient. Particularly on warm summer days, you must reach farther down – into deeper, and thus colder, water – in order to make contact with the fish. What you need is a sinking line, although the technique is essentially the same. The fly should be cast across the boat's drift direction and, when it has landed, you let out extra line so that it can sink to the right depth. The deeper it must go, the more time it must be given to descend, unless you switch to a faster sinking line.

Striking from a boat

Especially when fishing with a sinking line, you may find yourself keeping a rather long line out, together with the problems it entails. If you have 20-25 metres of elastic fly line out behind the boat, there can be difficulty in hooking fish – even from a drifting boat, which automatically helps to hook them.

Consequently, the strike is often decisive for whether a fish ends up in your boat. And a strike is not just an automatic lift of the rod tip. It is largely ineffective with a long, elastic line. Instead, you must ensure that the rod tip always points straight out towards the fly – if possible, with the tip guide in or under the water surface. And it should be there when the fish strikes! This can be difficult for many people to accept, as their reflexes from traditional fishing with dry flies and nymphs are hard to shake off. But it is definitely necessary for good results.

The rod tip should be in the water while your left hand pulls in the line and hooks the fish. This is the only secure means of hooking the fish, when you use a long line out to a streamer or bucktail. These are big flies tied on hefty hooks, which cannot automatically penetrate far into the jaws of trout. You have to assist them if you want any fish in your boat!

A desirable "hanger"

As a rule, when you flyfish from a drifting boat, the water beneath it is deep and it faces few obstacles. So this is a kind of fishing which poses no great problems for using more than one fly on your leader. Classic English boat fishing, as mentioned above, calls for three small wet flies. But we need not go that far with our big streamers or bucktails: a single fly is normally enough.

On the other hand, situations do arise where it is very rewarding to "hang" a little fly before the big

streamer. Both in lakes and at sea, trout are fond of a particular combination: a bushy Palmer fly on the bob, and a large luminous bucktail or streamer on the tail. This is supposed to imitate a small fish chasing an even smaller prey fish – something which often arouses envy in otherwise sluggish trout. The same is true of other fish species. Your little fly will frequently be taken by perch in lakes, and by garfish in the sea.

Drift-boat flyfishing is actually reminiscent of traditional downstream wet-fly fishing in a waterway. The difference is just that, in this case, the movement is done by the boat rather than the water. You can therefore mend your line "upstream" (with the wind)

or "downstream" (against the wind) in order to decrease or increase the fly's speed through the water, whenever necessary. Moreover, you can assist the fly by taking in line while the boat drifts, since it does so very slowly.

However, especially when you have to use a sinking line for reaching down to the fish, you can hardly fish effectively – at the right depth – in a short time. Mostly the fly is either on the way down to that depth, or on the way back up. Of course, if you want the fly to fish well for a long period, you can anchor the boat as described earlier, although this will limit the area of water that can be fished.

In traditional boat-fishing around the British Isles, the flies are presented with a float-line and short casts in the direction of drift. Streamers and bucktails, though, must be fished faster and possibly also deeper, so a sink-line may be very useful. Since you then often have a long line out, the rod tip must be aligned with the line – pointing toward the fly – to make the counter-strike effective. Keep in mind, too, that such big flies have strong hooks and may not hook the trout unless you lift the rod tip and pull on the line. A large, spacious landing-net will naturally increase your chances of final success.

Trolling with a fly

The last problem finds its solution in a method of fishing which has both staunch advocates and stubborn opponents. The enthusiasts explain that they can fish their flies at the correct depth all the time, whereas others complain that this should no longer be called true flyfishing.

Yes, it's the old trick of trolling – or trailing a fly after a moving boat. "Dull as dishwashing," in the words of some Englishmen. They may have a point, but the fact is as follows. If fish cannot be caught in the upper water layer, and are not even there, it will do little good to go on casting. Then you have to choose between playing golf or, by tying your fly on a sinking line, doing some trolling.

To believe that trolling with a fly involves simply tossing the fly into your propeller wash, and sailing around until a silly trout takes it, would be completely wrong. Certainly this can be done, and has been done by many people – without any imagination or insight. But such trollers are not experienced flyfishermen. The latter, instead, experiment with the proper fishing depth and use fly lines with different sinking speeds. There is no foolproof recipe for reaching the right depth with a trolling fly, and that's a good thing!

The depth at which a trolling fly really fishes is dependent on several factors. Among them are the boat's speed, the line's sinking speed, and the length of the line.

A short leader

Trolling is seldom done with either floating or intermediate lines. An exception is trolling in the late afternoon and night hours, when the fish gladly take at or near the surface. In daytime, it is almost always necessary to get farther down for contact with the fish. WF lines, such as Wet Cel II and Hi-D, are the most common for general trolling. On warm summer days, though, you may well profit from a Hi-Speed Hi-D line, or even a Deep Water Express. With these two, you should use shooting heads rather than a WF line, to maximize the fishing depth. In addition, the leader should not be more than a metre long.

Unless one goes to extremes, increasing the line length behind the boat will make the fly run deeper. With general WF lines, this applies up to 20-25 metres of length. With shooting heads that sink very fast on heavy shooting lines, you can use much greater

length and come even farther down. But the exact depth at which to fish will remain a mystery – unless you feel a solid bite at a known depth. Only then can you be sure, at least, that the fish swim so far down.

Trolling flies

A whole chapter could be devoted to trolling flies. The primary rule, though, is that they can hardly be too big. Monstrous flies, up to 4 inches (10 cm) long, are by no means excessive for large trout in deep water. In spite of this, most genuine flyfishermen tend to choose smaller flies that have won confidence in ordinary flyfishing. The result is a failure to make contact with the really large fish, which stay in waiting for sizable mouthfuls.

While the flies may be almost as big as you please, the hooks obviously can't. If you tie such a fighting fly on an ordinary streamer hook, the combination is so large that it will have trouble in hooking the fish securely.

This problem led American flyfishermen and flytiers, already at the beginning of our century, to tie tandem flies that could troll for large squaretail and

lake trout. These were long flies, normally with the tip turned upward on the rear hook, and downward in traditional fashion on the rear hook. A stiff steel wire linked the two hooks.

Flies of the same kind are used constantly today, but in the meantime we have acquired *tube flies*, which are no less effective. They can be tied very large without becoming heavy or clumsy. Their small treble hook gives a much better hold on the fish than do big single hooks. Tube flies tied on 2-inch (5-cm) tubing, with hairwings 4 inches (10 cm) long, are excellent trolling flies with loads of lovely trout on their consciences.

An overlooked method

The fly pattern is not a crucial factor, but the body should be made of tinsel or mylar, and the ample wing of long white hair. Then you have a highly edible fly, and a visible one in the water – just what you need for trolling at depth, neither more nor less.

It is quite permissible to place the fly rod in a rod-holder while fishing, and even to use several rods at the same time. But this definitely turns the sport into

something other than flyfishing – and diminishes the joy of seeing the regular, often violent, strikes that are offered by trolling. Nor does it allow you to give the extra pull which is frequently essential on a long line.

Trolling can be done from a rowing boat if you hold the rod clamped between your knees. Such a method is pleasant and commonly leaves you with a fish tearing the rod down onto the bottom-boards! At the opposite extreme, a motorboat can be used, but then you should give the fly extra life by continually feeding the line out and taking it in again. Finally, there is the passive form of trolling on a gusty day, by letting the boat drift as the fly fishes deep in its wake.

Without any doubt, trolling with a fly yields big fish. It must, too, be admitted that many flyfishermen dislike this method, and partly with good reason. Nonetheless, to ignore the whole approach would be a great mistake. If nothing else, trolling can be employed when you are moving from one fishing spot to another. Sooner or later, trailing the fly behind your boat will bring a strike, and not seldom from a very large fish. So think twice before writing off this way of fishing with streamers and bucktails!

A method that has won ever more followers is trolling with a fly and fly-rod. There are many ways to experiment with the right fishing depth, such as using fly-lines with different sinking speeds, or varying the line length and the boat's speed. When fishing for big trout, as is commonly done by this method, there may well be huge flies – 10 cm long or more – on the leader. Consequently, long hairwing tube flies, with a double or treble hook at the rear, are especially suitable. The flies must also be visible at great distances in the water, so they should contain bright and shiny materials. An example is the fly shown here (in natural size), with a body of mylar tubing and wings of long white hair.

The future of Trout Fishing

It is a thought-provoking fact that there are ever more fishermen going after the same fish in the same fishing waters. The pressure on nature is climbing day by day, and this cannot go on forever. Long past is the time when one could find solitude along a good stretch of fishing water amid undisturbed wildlife! And we must, in the end, get used to it.

Furthermore, we have to accept that an increasing number of restrictions will be placed on fishing in the future. Access to the most stressed - that is, popular - waters will be controlled, and limits will be put on both catches and fishing methods. All this has the good intention, of course, to enable nature to withstand the growing pressure on fish.

Therefore, it is very important for flyfishermen as a whole to take active part in campaigning for a better water environment - one which allows the trout to reproduce themselves, so that extensive and costly stocking becomes needless.

Already today, we can see how many neglected lakes and waterways have been recreated, their trout recovering natural conditions of life. Polluted waste water is cleaned before being led away, irrigation streams are restored to their old winding channels, the acidified lakes are limed, and so on.

Harmful stocking

Even the best fishing waters, with an optimal relationship between food supplies and spawning areas, can tolerate only a limited fishing pressure before they start to show signs of overfishing. As a result, the fish stocks must often be supported with some degree of restocking in order to stay intact. A key requirement is that this stocking has to come from the given water's own strain of fish, which has adapted itself for thousands of years to that water's particular character.

Randomly selected fish for stocking can be quite harmful, since they gradually "thin out" the original strain and its genetic traits. This is just what happens when cultivated fish are set out and mix with the wild fish in spawning areas.

Improved techniques of cultivation

Great efforts are being made today in many places to obtain the right kinds of breeding fish for farms, often on a voluntary unpaid basis. The fish are caught in traps or with electricity, and the roe and milt are squeezed out of those ready to spawn. The fertilized eggs are then kept in hatching vessels with running water, until they hatch and the young trout crawl out.

Cultivated fish may be set out as fry, or raised to become larger fish for implantation. The latter are set out after half a year, or one or two years, at suitable spots in the water system. Small fish are introduced in shallow waters, and large specimens farther downstream in deeper water. Silvery young fish (smolt) ready to migrate are often released fairly near the sea, where they quickly descend and swim away.

Even massive restocking is by no means always sufficient to save threatened stocks of trout. Frequently an extra effort is needed on the part of sportfishermen. For example, one of the most debated forms of nature conservation is "catch-and-release". The practice was borrowed from the United States, where it has been used for about thirty years, yielding substantial experience of this radical approach to fish management.

Wild fish and "tame" fish

At more and more places in the USA, Canada and Alaska, a sharp distinction is drawn between two kinds of fish. Wild fish are those hatched and raised in nature, while "tame" fish are stocked.

Wild fish are understandably regarded as much more valuable, since they have long been exposed to nature's merciless selection of the fittest to survive. Consequently, wild fish are far better adapted to the water systems they live in, than are temporarily visiting cultivated fish. Special regulations have thus been laid down for the benefit of wild fish. Among other things, they are entirely protected from fishing, and must be released if caught - unlike the cultivated fish, which can be taken for the creel.

For purposes of recognition, the cultivated fish are usually marked before being set out - for instance, by

If we are to experience unspoiled fishing for big trout in the future as well, it is clearly essential to protect the priceless natural resources that we borrow during our own time on Earth. Coming generations of flyfishermen will certainly also want to have a chance with trout in their proper environments – that is, clean undisturbed waters with ecologically intact surroundings and a pristine, flourishing insect fauna...

clipping off the adipose fin. If one then catches fish with a clipped-off fin, one knows that they can be killed and retained.

In addition, by establishing a minimum size for kept fish, it is possible to ensure that the fish will survive and become large enough to spawn at least once, making a contribution to the survival of their strain. Unfortunately, the introduction of a fixed minimum size also means that only a few fish in the water will be much larger than the minimum, since the fish are mostly caught and killed as soon as they exceed that critical level.

Consistent fish management

Waters with strong fishing pressure, therefore, tend to have almost no big fish. At many places, for example in Alaska where the spawning opportunities are good, a so-called maximum size has thus been introduced instead. It means that you can only catch and kill fish which are below a limit such as 20 inches (50 cm). This policy guarantees that large fish will also be pre-

sent, as long as their natural production by spawning is great enough.

Sportfishermen obviously are most interested in big fish, which also are the most important in spawning areas. The full consequences of this development have been taken, in ever more parts of North America, by introducing concepts like "no-kill" and "catch-and-

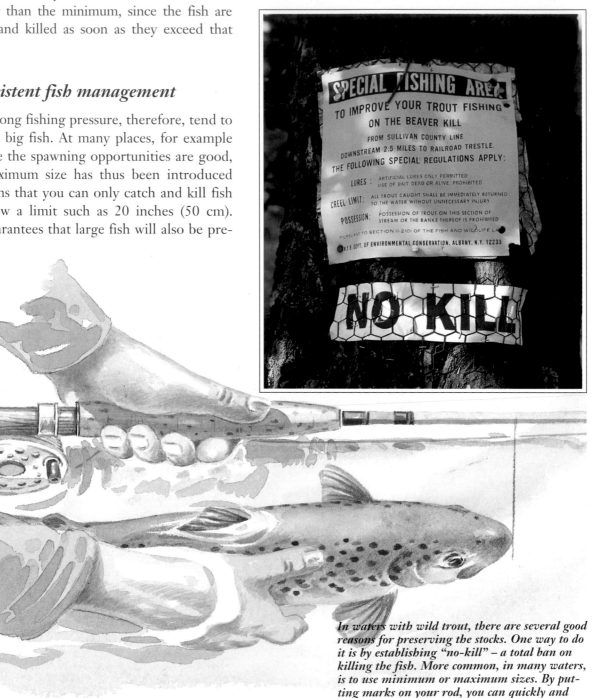

In waters with wild trout, there are several good reasons for preserving the stocks. One way to do it is by establishing "no-kill" – a total ban on killing the fish. More common, in many waters, is to use minimum or maximum sizes. By putting marks on your rod, you can quickly and easily tell the length of a caught fish.

release" to rational fish management. In these waters, one can only fish with barbless single hooks, and all fish must be set out again. Repeated studies have shown that fish which are caught and released in the right way have very good chances of survival, and that virtually none of them die as a direct result of the fishing.

It has quite often turned out that, after the introduction of catch-and-release fishing, the stocks multiply several times and include more big fish than previously. In other words, they become much more attractive stocks, at least for us flyfishermen.

Put-and-take fishing

Where trout are concerned, the measures in many countries are divided into three aspects. First we have the outright put-and-take waters, where cultivated large fish are set out for the sole purpose of being caught again as soon as possible. This is called "intensive" put-and-take fishing.

At the same time, there is "extensive" put-and-take fishing, in which cultivated small fish are set out in order to grow and reach catchable sizes. This is common in private put-and-take waters with low fishing pressure and a correspondingly high quality of both fish and fishing techniques. It also occurs frequently with two of our most popular sportfish - salmon and sea trout.

In regard to sea trout, the natural reproduction today is often exceedingly small, due to the destruction of spawning areas together with the inadequate accessibility of those that remain. If there were not massive implantations, primarily of young fish, we would actually have poor fishing for sea trout along the coasts. Hence, sea trout can be taken with a clear conscience, if they meet the minimum size requirement and are not caught during times of protection.

Finally, there are the stationary stocks in waterways

In flowing waters, an abundance of spawning beds usually means a lot of small trout. If such bottoms are rare, the fish tend to be fewer but larger. Thus the supply of spawning beds will govern the stock's composition.

- mainly trout and grayling. The latter are still naturally self-reproducing in many places. These stationary fish are often found in limited sections of water, but are also subject to heavy fishing pressure, not least in streams where day-permits are sold.

An unsatisfactory situation

The last-mentioned fish could easily be fished to extinction if restrictions on fishing did not exist. This is why the stocks are frequently supplemented today with regular implantations of catchable trout from pond farms. But these hardly have time to acclimatize themselves before being caught again. The drawbacks of such a procedure should be evident to serious and environmentally minded sportfishermen, who want to catch wild fish under conditions as natural as possible.

Apart from restoration of spawning grounds and improved access to them, there is only one thing to do: introduce "no-kill" and "catch- and-release". No other kind of fish management is able to give us natural stocks of wild brown trout in many overfished waters.

In northern Sweden, the opposite problem often arises, and precisely with brown trout. The opportunities for spawning are so good in many places that there are too many trout. Since the food supply is frequently quite limited in mountain streams and rivers, the result is a vast stock of small fish that grow slowly. Thus, not only can one take home a catch with a clear conscience - one ought to do so, in the interests of fish management! The stock should be thinned out so that the remaining fish have a chance to get bigger.

At Yellowstone National Park, it was soon realised that the ever greater fishing pressure would create an impossible situation. The result was, first, a ban on fishing with live bait – then a minimum size of 35 cm, followed by catch-and-release as well as no-kill. Not least the stocks of gluttonous cutthroat trout (inset at right) responded very positively to these limits, increasing both their numbers and average size.

The history of no-kill fishing

The first official happy catch-and-release tale came from Yellowstone National Park. This park, also the first of its kind in the world, was established in 1872. Until the beginning of our century, only 5-10,000 people visited it each year.

But the stream of tourists swelled to more than 65,000 annually at the end of World War II, and to over 2.5 million by about 1970! Only then did it become plain that restrictions were needed to prevent the pressure of so many visitors from disturbing the unique natural surroundings and their permanent population.

Among the park's unique inhabitants, there is still a

special strain of "cutthroat" trout - a close relative of the rainbow trout. In Yellowstone Lake and its outflow, the Yellowstone River, the cutthroat came under hard pressure from several quarters. Some were the other inhabitants: grizzly bears, mink and eagle, as well as a colony of white pelicans which, all by themselves, took no fewer than 300-400,000 fully grown trout per year. Also present are visiting sportfishermen who, during a three-month period in 1970, ran up a total of 370,000 fishing days and caught an estimated 300,000 fish. The park managers realized that something radical had to be done before the entire local ecosystem collapsed.

New restrictions

Until World War II, the increasing pressure on fish had been compensated for, by setting out ever more fish - specifically, cultivated fish of unknown origin. This faunal pollution stopped already in 1950, though, because of the desire to preserve the park's original stock of wild fish.

It was also clear to the management that an immediate, absolute introduction of catch-and-release fishing would provoke an outcry from the park's guests. Instead, restrictions were gradually strengthened during a three-year period. First, fishing with natural bait was forbidden, since investigations had revealed that it causes death in 50-70% of the caught and released fish, compared to only 5-10% with artificial bait.

Next, for the first time in the park's history, a minimum length of 14 inches (35 cm) was introduced for cutthroat trout. From 1955 until 1968, there had been a catch limit of two fish per person daily in Yellowstone Lake - based on the lake's productivity and moderate fishing pressure. But when the rising pressure for four years in a row had exceeded the level of what the lake could tolerate, fishing completely collapsed. It was then that the minimum length succeeded in decreasing the annual catch by about 100,000 fish.

Learning from mistakes

Moreover, the water system began to teem with small first-time spawners. The older age groups, on the other hand - those above the minimum length - quickly disappeared. As soon as they reached that length, they were caught and consumed.

This imbalance displeased the park managers, who wanted to offer visitors a natural kind of fishing for natural stocks that could include large and attractive specimens. To equalize the numbers of big and small fish, catch-and-release as well as absolute no-kill fishing were introduced in 1972.

The effects were impressive. Over a four-year period, the fish increased in both number and size. Ironically, once-critical sportfishermen were now heard asking the park management why this had not been done earlier! The catch-and-release waters became the most frequently visited of all.

When the ban on natural bait was first applied, a correspondingly lower pressure on the fish was observed - the reason being simply that those who fished with natural bait stayed away. However, the catch-and-release waters regained their popularity due to the new quality fishing, which could boast plentiful and sizable wild fish.

It was discovered that greedy species of trout, such as the brook trout and cutthroat, reacted quite positively to catch-and-release. For relatively shy species like rainbow trout and brown trout, the results were different. These also responded with more and larger fish, but not very noticeably from the viewpoint of sportfishermen. Rainbow, and especially brown trout, learn rapidly from their mistakes. Ultimately, therefore, they can be caught only by the most adept fishermen.

Nonetheless, in terms of fish biology, catch-and-release is definitely to the advantage of all trout stocks that are exposed to hard fishing pressure.

Correct releasing

The example of Yellowstone, while not unique, has served as a model for other places during the past decade or so. Yet if catch-and-release is to give the desired results, a requirement must be fulfilled: the caught fish have to be released in the right way. This calls for a certain insight and understanding of how fish function. If they are handled improperly, a fair number of them die after being released. Otherwise the toll will be negligible - only a few percent.

Short performances

Fish and humans behave differently under physical pressure. Unlike us, fish are not suited to making continuous, long, hard physical efforts. In most fish - not least the trout - only a small part of the musculature consists of so-called red muscles. This part is what enables a mammal, such as ourselves, to perform heavy work for long periods.

Instead, a fish primarily contains white muscles, a kind that is very well adapted to brief, sprinter-like activities, such as forcing powerful rapids and leaping over waterfalls. Between these sudden displays of strength, fish have to rest adequately. Unless they do, lactic-acid poisoning will put an end to them.

The same process is familiar from our own experience. If we overwork our muscles, perhaps due to lack of exercise, they become stiff and tender, because of accumulated lactic acid. This substance is formed when the normal metabolism is deficient in energy - that is, when the muscles work harder than the oxygen supply allows. Lactic acid then steps in as a kind of

Unlike human beings, trout cannot take long periods of hard physical stress without lactic-acid poisoning. Therefore, trout must not be played any longer than necessary – regardless of whether they are to be released – since their chances of survival will otherwise sink drastically. Neither should too light equipment be used, as it prolongs the fight.

substitute metabolism, which gives extra energy but only on borrowed time. The "acid debt" must be repaid with poorer muscle function.

If you want to memorialize a truly beautiful fish, such as a "trophy trout", it should be lifted up quickly and photographed, then lowered back into the water.
Do not hold it too tightly or with dry hands, lest you damage its innards or protective slime layer, respectively.

Fatal poisoning

Matters are even worse for a fish, since it has proportionately fewer red muscles - lying in a small band along the lateral line. There are, of course, exceptions. The family of tuna, as well as sailfish, marlin and swordfish, have more red muscles, so they possess great stamina and are fast long-distance swimmers.

The predominantly white muscles of salmonoids make them especially sensitive to long periods of physical exertion. A large trout, that can easily leap over a waterfall two metres high, has no chance in an hour-long fight with a sportfisherman. It is doomed to defeat, not by the fisherman's superior intelligence or strength, but by its own overproduction of lactic acid.

An interesting fact in this context is that death from lactic acid in the blood does not occur instantly. Instead, the accumulation takes place in steps, during

three to twelve hours after the exertion. So even if the fish manages to swim away after a long fight, it may die of the consequences.

Main rules for catch-and-release

• Use appropriate equipment! With tackle that is too light, you will prolong the fight, allowing the fish's lactic-acid content to become needlessly high.

• Fight the fish fast, under constant pressure! Thus you can avoid letting the production of lactic acid in the fish become greater than absolutely necessary. In other words, don't play with your prey.

• Do not hold the fish too hard! A fish is suited to a weightless life underwater, where the inner organs are not subject to significant pressure. Small fish often become calmer if held over the back, with the belly upward, while the hook is loosened.

• Try to use barbless hooks! These enable you to free a landed fish quickly from the hook. If the hook sits deep, leave it there and cut off the line. It will either rust to pieces or become overgrown and harmless. Never attempt to rip it out. A fish that is bleeding from the gills or throat will probably die. Long-shanked pliers (surgical forceps) are essential for rapidly and effectively removing hooks from fish.

• Avoid catch-and-release fishing or practising in summer-warm water! There is much less oxygen in warm water than in cold water, while the fish's metabolism requires comparatively more oxygen in warm water. Hence, a fish that is fought and released in warm water faces a much higher risk of dying from oxygen-poor lactic-acid poisoning than do fish in cold water.

• Do not lift the fish out of the water! Recent studies have shown that even a short time (30-60 seconds) out of water will markedly increase fatality after release. If you want to photograph the fish, this should be done in just a few seconds.

• Avoid touching the fish with dry hands! Either dry hands or a dry landing-net will damage the fish's protective layer of mucus, and render it more vulnerable to fungi and bacteria. Thus you should not, if possible, net the fish. A net made of soft cotton without knots is ideal, unlike nylon nets with knots.

• Give the fish artificial respiration before releasing it! Once the hook is removed, the fish must be revived. If you are fishing in a waterway, hold the fish with its head against the current, so that fresh water runs in through the gills. When the gills start to work regularly and the fish can keep its balance, it is ready for release.

In lakes and other still waters, give artificial respiration by moving the fish back and forth in the water. The fish should be able to swim by itself from your hands, before it is ready to be released. If it turns its belly upward despite several minutes of artificial respiration, it will not survive.

Sensitive creatures

The difficulty of reviving a fish after a long fight varies widely between kinds of fish. Trout and char are generally in much better condition than grayling and whitefish, which can be hard to revive. But this is not all. Fish can behave differently according to the season, and to whether they are coloured (ready for spawning) or silvery (sexually mature).

After a violent battle, a silvery fresh-run trout may be almost impossible to revive. Its physiology is an obstacle to its survival, and it might be compared to a fast sports car or a thoroughbred horse - quick at the start, but queasy at the end.

By contrast, mature spawning fish in streams or rivers are fairly rugged. They are migrating to reproduce in their own waterways, where their bodies are prepared for rough encounters with waterfalls that must be forced, or sharp cliffs that can rip their skins. Strong spawning "costumes" - tough skin and a thick layer of mucus - are the gifts with which nature has adapted the fish to these conditions.

The wisdom of moderation

Whatever we do to prevent them, some fatalities are inevitable when catching and releasing fish. And a death rate of just a few percent can have a huge impact on the fish stocks, if the fishing pressure is high enough.

Not even on a day when the air is full of swarming insects, and the trout are going crazy on the surface, is there any excuse for catching and releasing fish until your arms nearly fall off. You would then cause the death of far more fish than necessary. Today, you have an improved opportunity of showing moderation and respect toward nature - by instead wading ashore and enjoying the scenery, without fishing at all!

Perhaps in the future, restrictions will be made for catch-and-release fishing. Will they add a limit of, say, only five fish per day? This would be both a reasonable development of the concept, and a benefit to our fish stocks.

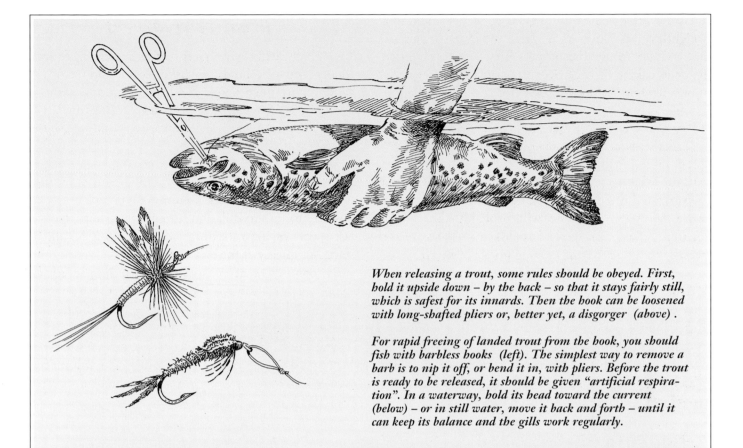

When releasing a trout, some rules should be obeyed. First, hold it upside down – by the back – so that it stays fairly still, which is safest for its innards. Then the hook can be loosened with long-shafted pliers or, better yet, a disgorger (above) .

For rapid freeing of landed trout from the hook, you should fish with barbless hooks (left). The simplest way to remove a barb is to nip it off, or bend it in, with pliers. Before the trout is ready to be released, it should be given "artificial respiration". In a waterway, hold its head toward the current (below) – or in still water, move it back and forth – until it can keep its balance and the gills work regularly.

Index